Each day, it seemed, we'd lose another piece of Phil. . . .There was no end to it, and I remember thinking that no one else could see what I see. No one knew what it was like, to be caught up in it like we were. We had an amazing group of supportive friends, and our families couldn't have been more caring, but it's a lonely thing to be married to a man in the depths of a depression with an infant daughter at home. . . . It was all about getting through each day.

I'd never felt more alone.

—From *Morning Has Broken*

"I was so inspired by this story of love, courage, and stead-fastness which came shining through the struggle of Emme and Phil and their family. Clinical depression is such an insidious, potentially life-threatening illness, and Emme's and Phil's courageous and honest willingness to share their story can help and encourage many millions of couples and families. It is an astonishingly candid and clear description of the suffering felt by both people when depression is present in a relationship. They persevered through many different treatments and allow us to feel not only their moments of despair and anguish, but more important, their hope, joy, and love for each other. This is a story of the triumph of the human spirit, and it is an illuminating window into the reality of day-to-day dealing with the illness that is depression."

—Tipper Gore

continued . . .

"Emme and Phil's was a journey through the very portals of hell, one that ultimately affirms something that anyone who struggles with depression needs to know—depression isn't a dead end. It just feels that way. The couple's story is one of pain, power, perseverance, love—and hope."

—Dr. Joseph J. Luciani, author of *Self-Coaching: How to Heal Anxiety and Depression*

Morning Has Broken

A COUPLE'S JOURNEY THROUGH DEPRESSION

EMME AND PHILLIP ARONSON

 NEW AMERICAN LIBRARY

New American Library
Published by New American Library, a division of
Penguin Group (USA) Inc., 375 Hudson Street,
New York, New York 10014, USA
Penguin Group (Canada), 90 Eglinton Avenue East, Suite 700, Toronto,
Ontario M4P 2Y3, Canada (a division of Pearson Penguin Canada Inc.)
Penguin Books Ltd., 80 Strand, London WC2R 0RL, England
Penguin Ireland, 25 St. Stephen's Green, Dublin 2,
Ireland (a division of Penguin Books Ltd.)
Penguin Group (Australia), 250 Camberwell Road, Camberwell, Victoria 3124,
Australia (a division of Pearson Australia Group Pty. Ltd.)
Penguin Books India Pvt. Ltd., 11 Community Centre, Panchsheel Park,
New Delhi - 110 017, India
Penguin Group (NZ), cnr Airborne and Rosedale Roads, Albany,
Auckland 1310, New Zealand (a division of Pearson New Zealand Ltd.)
Penguin Books (South Africa) (Pty.) Ltd., 24 Sturdee Avenue,
Rosebank, Johannesburg 2196, South Africa

Penguin Books Ltd., Registered Offices:
80 Strand, London WC2R 0RL, England

Published by New American Library, a division of Penguin Group (USA) Inc.
Previously published in a New American Library hardcover edition.

First New American Library Trade Paperback Printing, January 2007
10 9 8 7 6 5 4 3 2

■ REGISTERED TRADEMARK—MARCA REGISTRADA
New American Library Trade Paperback ISBN: 978-0-451-21962-6

The Library of Congress has cataloged the hardcover edition of this title as follows:

Aronson, Emme.
Morning has broken: a couple's journey through depression/Emme and
Phillip Aronson.
p. cm.
ISBN 0-451-21807-8 (hardcover)
1. Depression, Mental.   2. Depression, Mental—Patients—Family
relationships.   I. Aronson, Phillip.   II. Title.
RC537.A76 2006
616.85'270092—dc22   2005026843

Set in Palatino
Designed by Ginger Legato

Printed in the United States of America

TO JONATHAN

Your support, strength and never-ending love
during *your* most difficult times will never be forgotten.

You are our light.

We miss you.

"Knock me down, but don't count me out."

—Unknown

CONTENTS

CONTENTS

Morning Has Broken

OPENING THOUGHTS

Life, Interrupted

PHIL

I used to sit at the edge of my bed for hours and hours, or look at myself in the bathroom mirror until I no longer recognized the face staring back at me. I couldn't follow a simple conversation. I had a brand-new baby daughter, and I could barely pay attention to her; I missed her first words, her first steps, her first everything. I wouldn't bathe for days on end. I took no interest in work, or sex, or friends and family. I talked constantly about killing myself, and it wasn't just talk: I tempted fate so often it's a wonder I'm still alive.

And yet here I am, alive and thriving, two years removed from a debilitating depression that nearly cost me everything, and as I look back on my ordeal I can't help but feel empowered. Emboldened. Enriched, even. I know it sounds like a line, but it's the God's honest truth. I've been to hell and back, and I'm a better person for it. I'm open to people and ideas and relationships in new and exciting ways. I'm open to possibility. Plus, I'm so much more appreciative of everything life has to offer—everything *my* life has to offer—because I now know what it's like to turn away from those gifts. You know how it is when you've been away from home for a long time, and that first night back in your own bed is just total bliss? Well, that's kind of what the past two years have been like for me, and I'm hoping I'll feel that way for the rest of my life. Like I'm back in my own bed after a long, difficult journey.

This is a book about depression. More to the point, it's a book about *surviving* depression. It's a book about how my wife, Emme, and I managed together to overcome a serious mental illness that pretty much derailed our lives, and at the same time it serves as a guide for other couples going through their own versions of the same ordeal. I'm betting (hoping!) that a lot of you picked up this book because of Emme. She's the hot-looking babe on the book jacket cover. I'm the not-so-hot-looking guy to her left. As a lot of you already know, Emme's helped a great many people get past a variety of body-image and self-esteem issues, but what you probably don't know is how critically helpful she was to me in overcoming my depression. It pulled her away from her modeling career, and her ability to spread the good word on the lecture circuit, but she was a relentless angel. I would not be here to write these words were it not for her unflagging love and support and care, and when we emerged on the healing end of this ordeal, it occurred to us we had an all-important message to share for couples going through a depression. It's a giant big deal—for patient and caregiver alike—and we caught ourselves thinking we were now uniquely positioned to help couples on each end of the depression equation.

Please realize, we don't come to these pages from a place of expertise. We don't pretend to know all the answers. In fact, there were times when things were at their very worst when we didn't even know what questions to ask, or where to turn, all of which eventually got us thinking there was a real need for a straight-talking, no-nonsense primer for couples on what it takes to see your way to the other side of a clinical depression. Really, it would have made our ordeal so much more *navigable* if there'd been a set of CliffsNotes on how to survive depression, or some kind of guide (*Depression for Dummies*?) to offer us the benefit of someone else's insight and experience.

Before the depression found us, we had made it our business to spread a different kind of message—namely, that the human body comes in all shapes and sizes and that we should find ways to feel good about ourselves no matter what shape or size we happen to be. That was Emme's calling, as the world's leading full-figured model, and it became mine as well, as Emme's manager. Our work was endlessly rewarding, and after we'd been at it a while we became fairly expert on eating disorders and related body-image and self-esteem issues. I have to admit, Emme was a little more expert than yours truly, but even I got to where I really knew my stuff, and that's what we're after here, spreading what we believe is a positive, hopeful message that's just as powerful and promises to help just as many people.

It's a whole new arena for us, and we certainly don't

intend to pass ourselves off as authorities, but there's no denying that we're survivors. And we're not alone. According to the National Institute of Mental Health, 18.5 million Americans suffer each year from clinical depression. That's one in six adults! And more than 32 million Americans will experience a major depressive disorder in their lifetimes. The entire constellation of mood disorders, which includes bipolar disorder—also known as manic depression and characterized by extreme changes in mood, thought, energy and behavior—refuses to distinguish among class, age, race, gender or ethnicity. It's an equal-opportunity illness, open to all comers. It doesn't matter if you're the CEO of a Fortune 500 company or a shift worker on a loading dock— it can find you and set you reeling. And it can find you again and again: of those who get through a depression, about 40 percent will experience a subsequent depression at some point in their lifetimes. (Yes, I know . . . that sucks, but everything about depression sucks, doesn't it?)

These are huge numbers, and yet most of these good people are suffering in silence. Why? Well, sad to say, folks just don't talk about depression. They should, but they don't. That's one of the reasons why we couldn't find a book like this one when we went looking. For all of our progress and openness as a society, mental health issues remain very much a private, sweep-it-under-the-rug matter— that is, until recently, when celebrities like Brooke Shields and Lorraine Bracco moved out in front in discussing their battles with depression. Still, we're a long way from a climate where people will be encouraged to share their experiences with depression the way they would talk about cancer, or multiple sclerosis, or heart disease. It's kind of like divorce, back when we were growing up: there's a stigma to it, a taint, an unspoken belief that it should be . . . well, unspoken. People are ashamed of being perceived as weak, but Emme and I see ourselves as stronger for having been through it, and we intend to share some of that strength and positivity with anyone who cares to listen. The hushed topic of mental health ought to be a front-burner issue in our society, right alongside the lack of health insurance coverage for children and families, and the hard-to-shake social stigma that comes with treatments like electroconvulsive therapy (ECT) and certain antidepressants, and we want to address those issues here.

What is clinical depression? Simply put, it's an illness that affects mind and body in pretty much equal measure. It can leave sufferers with difficulty handling everyday situations and routines, to the extreme point where suicide might loom as the only perceived way to alleviate the anguish and confusion. It's linked to an imbalance in two of the human body's naturally occurring chemicals—serotonin and norepinephrine—which help to regulate how we process thoughts and feelings.

Happily, depression can be treated, and there have been some tremendous advances in recent years, particularly in the areas of medication and other aggressive forms of treatment. Many of the medications are intended to restore the balance to the body's serotonin and norepinephrine levels, while others are meant as mood enhancers or mood restorers. In my case, some worked and some didn't. Some worked for just a short while, before proving ineffective.

Some took a long time before showing any results. With me, it took months of stops and starts before my doctors hit on an effective treatment plan, and even then there were another few months of tweaks and adjustments.

In this one respect, at least, my depression was typical: there's no one medication or "cocktail" of medications that is guaranteed to work effectively in every case; each individual is different, and each "imbalance" is different, and it can take a good long while for doctors to discover the right combination of medications for any one person. The same holds true for the variety of alternative treatments that are now widely available, up to and including the electroconvulsive therapy I ultimately received. Sometimes these treatments work, and sometimes they don't—but the trick, we learned, is to keep trying anything and everything until your symptoms are under control, and eventually until they disappear entirely.

Everyone is different, and every depression is different. The common denominator is that depression touches every part of your life. It can change or influence your moods, your thoughts, your behavior, or the way you interact with colleagues, friends and family. It can set your relationships on edge, or leave you feeling weak and tired, or with aches and pains you've never experienced before. Some people report feeling endlessly overwhelmed, or sad, or stressed, meaning that their symptoms are mostly emotional. Others report symptoms that are mostly physical, such as fatigue, chronic pain or migraine headaches. And still others suffer symptoms that are emotional *and* physical.

Not surprisingly, there's a genetic component to most

mental illnesses, meaning that people with a family history of depression might be more prone to it themselves, but anyone can find themselves in a depression, at any time. Here, too, I fit the profile: the Aronson family tree is lined with aunts and cousins and grandparents who struggled through some of these same paces, and on the very closest limb there's my identical twin brother, Seth, who suffered a serious bout of depression in his early twenties.

Of course, the roots of depression are not purely genetic; it can be caused by a variety of "stressors" and other factors. Sometimes the trigger can be external, such as relationship troubles or financial difficulties; sometimes the trigger can be internal, such as a physical illness, or sleep deprivation, or a sudden hormonal shift, or an old athletic injury that never got the proper attention the first time around; and sometimes there's no clear trigger at all. We'll never be entirely sure about the cause of my depression, but the effect was certainly clear: it very nearly cost us everything, and when we were in the middle of it we never knew how our story might turn out.

Now, from a place of health and healing, we're finally able to look back at our ordeal and put it into some kind of perspective. Together we hope to shine an empowering light on an illness that demands our full attention, and together we pray that our shared struggle might present a path that others might follow. Our goal here is to reassure readers suffering through a depression or caring for someone suffering through a depression that they are not alone, or crazy, or without hope. There have been books and survival journals written about depression, and some of them are very good, but we've yet to come across a frank account of what it takes for a couple to withstand the ordeal, and that's what we're after here. We want to show how things were for *us*.

And just how *were* things, in a nutshell? Frankly, we were a mess, but once I came out of it and began to heal, my good friend Todd encouraged me to turn my mess into a message. So here goes, with the hope that readers take away the clear message that depression is *not* a sign of personal weakness, and that it *cannot* be willed or wished away, and that well-meaning friends and family who encourage you to "just snap out of it" simply don't know what they're talking about.

Sometimes it's hard to dig deep. There are thoughts and observations we have trouble letting into our own heads, let alone sharing with complete strangers. And that could have been how I chose to play it, after my depression lifted, but nothing seemed more important than sharing my story— *our* story. We could have been fence sitters, and shared nothing of what we'd been through, but we're sharing our story to remind fellow sufferers that suicide is a permanent solution to what is a decidedly temporary problem. We're sharing our story so others will understand that they are not alone, and that they can choose to live and not fall prey to the darkness of depression.

We're sharing our story so we can make a difference.

We're sharing our story so I can rationalize why I was so sick in the first place—and so Emme can give voice and strength to the legion of spouses and partners caught in the overwhelming role of caregiver.

We're sharing our story because we've heard from thousands of people—no exaggeration!—who reached out to us with letters and e-mails of encouragement, gratitude and support, after we submitted to a major profile in *People* magazine in March 2005 that chronicled our nightmare in our own words.

We're sharing our story because everywhere we go these days we hear from someone who's got a spouse, or an aunt, or a cousin, or a sibling, or a best friend who's been in a depression, and they find in us kindred spirits who might be in a position to offer support—or maybe they just feel like talking. And Emme—bless her!—is sharing her take on the same ordeal so that the families and friends of depressed loved ones get the all-important message to hang tough and strong, along with some equally important encouragement to dig deep and discover their untapped well-springs of love, courage and support.

We're sharing our story because it can be a lonely, terrifying thing to care for someone trapped in a depression—oftentimes as lonely and terrifying as the depression itself.

We're sharing our story because life is short.

We're sharing our story because all daughters should have fathers.

We're sharing our story because we have to.

And we're sharing our story because we can. Thank God for that.

Prologue: August 1, 2003

EMME

It started with an argument—or, I should say, it nearly ended with an argument. That's how it was, and that's how I think back on it, when I relive the events of that horrific, life-changing day.

We had just come from the therapist's office the afternoon before. It was the first time during this whole ordeal that I had made an effort to look after me. It had taken me a while, but I'd finally realized I needed some kind of lifeline, some way to deal with what Phil's depression was doing to me as well as to him. I was worn down, and desperate for some kind of help. What I felt I needed most of all was to talk to someone who wasn't all wrapped up in Phil's treatment, someone whose knee-jerk response wouldn't be to tell me to hang in there. That was always the message: suck it up, give it some time, do the best you can, be strong for Phil. Every time I heard something like that I wanted to scream. Doctors, family, friends . . . they were all just trying to be supportive, but I was beyond supporting. I was drained, and hopeless, and impatient. Of course, I knew that these people were all well intentioned, and I guess I would have been the same way if I'd been on the outside looking in, but I wanted them to live under my roof, to sleep in my bed, to see what it was like to care for a man in the throes of a depression nobody seemed to want to do anything about, and at the same time care for our infant daughter. I wanted them to understand. I needed them to get that I was trying to hang in there but that it was impossible. I had been strong for Phil, for the longest time, and it had gotten us nowhere. I had given it time, and sucked it up, and everything else that was reasonably expected of me, but there was no relief, and no end in sight.

I didn't know where to get my air.

At this point in his illness, Phil couldn't be left alone, and needed to go with me everywhere I went, so he sat outside the door to my therapist's office, hearing God knows what coming through the door. I worried about that, even as I was in the middle of my session, although I doubt if anything I said could have penetrated his depression; he was so out of it, staring off into space, lost in his own thoughts, or not thinking anything at all, that I can't imagine anything really registered, even if he heard all of it.

My psychiatrist was a colleague of Phil's doctor, who had made the referral. I thought it was important for me to see someone outside Phil's circle of support, because I needed a sounding board that wasn't all caught up in Phil's care. I was angry. At the world. At Phil. At his doctors. At myself. And I needed a place to put that anger, but my precious forty-five minutes seemed to fly by like no time at all. Really, when I looked up from my talking and crying it felt like just ten minutes had passed, but my time was up. I felt like saying, "Is that all there is?" I felt cheated, like there had been no opportunity for any real give-and-take between me and the doctor—which I guess is one of the reasons I only went to see her that one time.

Anyway, I left the office on a kind of knife edge, with all that anger still very much at the surface, and I didn't have the patience for poor Phil at just that moment. I was horrible. I'm ashamed to admit it now, but I have to be honest. I took one look at my husband, slumped in that waiting room chair, looking all hangdog and defeated and so totally not like the man I'd married, and I thought, *Oh, great. Nothing's changed. Nothing's ever going to change.* The last thing I needed, I thought at the time, was to have to deal with Phil, who seemed willfully slumped in his chair, like he was making a point that I was not paying attention to him while I was inside the therapist's office, taking care of myself.

Clearly, I had a totally despairing attitude, which wasn't typical of me, but I'd shot past typical a couple months earlier. This was new territory. It was an especially low moment for me, coming out of that therapist's office, because it was obvious that it was another in a series of low moments for Phil, and there were no signs that they were going to lift any time soon. His low moments were now mine, and they were pressing in on me like a vise. I didn't like how they left me with all these feelings of anger and sadness and uncertainty. Phil no longer looked like the man I'd married.

His mannerisms seemed to belong to someone else. His expressions were all different. His moods were unrecognizable. He was on so many different medications, with so many different side effects, we needed a notebook just to keep track of them all, and every few days it seemed we were trying to adjust his meds and figure a combination that would actually work.

But I'd almost gotten used to Phil's new moods and mannerisms. The real kicker was that I had seemed to change. I no longer recognized myself. I wasn't the positive, joyful person I'd always tried to be. For as long as I could remember, I'd been a high-octane, high-energy person, with enthusiasm bursting from every pore, and that was all gone. I couldn't remember the last time I'd laughed. I couldn't even sleep at night. I used to concentrate on relaxing different body parts so I could fall asleep, and I always saved my face for last, because it needed the most work. I spent each day all twisted up inside, and I must have worn a look of constant worry, because it seemed like it took hours each night just to relax all those tense muscles in my face to where I could finally succumb to sleep.

You have to realize, I had always been a pretty patient person—my friends will tell you it's one of my strongest suits (at least I hope that's what they'll say!)—but whatever patience I'd had going into this thing was by now pretty much sapped, and I tried to hurry Phil to the car so we could get home and relieve the babysitter. It had been a lousy day going into this therapy session. I had just heard that our first clothing collection was being discontinued, so that had sent me reeling in a whole other direction, and now I'd put myself through these difficult motions with a new therapist, and it felt like I had cried out all my energy. All I could think of, at that moment, was getting home. That was my priority right then, but Phil was moving so slowly I wanted to just shake him. He moved like a man fifty years his senior, and a part of me felt like he was taunting me with how slowly he was moving, and I got so irritated that I just shouted, "Come on, Phil!" Like he was egging me on, and I was scolding him.

It took forever to get to the car, and while we were out on the street a man walked by with a dog on a leash, and it was like a light switched on in Phil's head. All of a sudden, he was back to his old self, stopping to pet the dog, asking perfectly appropriate questions of the man. He was up, and on, and totally in the moment. It was a side of him I hadn't seen in months, and at any other time it would have been a welcome sight, but just then it set me off. I became incensed that he could turn on for a complete stranger, but not for me, or his daughter, or anyone close to him. He could make the effort for someone he'd never see again, but not for his own family. It told me he could put on a brave, public face when he felt he needed to, and it pissed me off that he never felt he needed to when it was just us.

The guy walking the dog must have thought I was the one on medication, because I snapped at Phil like you wouldn't believe. "Get in the car now!" I screamed, and I hated how I sounded. Really, I was just so nasty, and I heard my voice and thought, *Oh, Emme, look what you've become.*

I couldn't keep my feelings in check. I couldn't just snap my fingers and chase away the anger, the frustration, the hopelessness. Those negative emotions bubbled to the surface and lingered a while, like ripples in a pond, and I knew myself well enough to realize they would take a while to disappear.

We didn't talk on the way home, and when we got to the house we went our separate ways. I needed time to cool off. I don't know what Phil needed. I couldn't even say for sure that my little tantrum registered with him in any kind of substantive way. For all I knew, he was off in his own zone, lost in whatever thoughts might manage to snake their way through his medications. Maybe Phil had the right idea, I thought, to set that low moment aside and make like it never happened, so that's what I tried to do, as soon as we got back to the house.

I spent some time with our daughter, Toby—our ray of sunshine. It's amazing, the guaranteed punch of acceptance when you walk into a room and get this unconditional love and pure, innocent joy from your child. Ah, and when she was just out of the bath, and freshly scrubbed and delicious . . . man, that was just the best. I could soak in Toby's sweetness and light and lose whatever it was that was contributing to my bad day. I lost myself in giving her something to eat, watching her happily struggle to place the spoon in or near her mouth. I loved watching all of her first-time, "big girl" moments, which helped to take me away from the weary routine of what the rest of my life had become, to where it took just a few minutes with her before my spirits began to lift and I could chase away the stresses of the day.

When I finally got Toby down to sleep, I tried to take

care of a few things around the house. After a while, I had calmed down enough to reach back out to Phil. I was determined to be rational, and strong, and to take care of my husband. Our world was fragile enough without any petty bickering, or the nonsense that sometimes passes between two people. The thing to do was to put the afternoon behind us, and move on, so with this in mind I asked Phil if he wanted to come into the den to watch television. He didn't answer. I asked him if he wanted me to fix him something to eat. He didn't answer, but I fixed him something anyway, and left it out for him in case he got hungry. Then I tried to lose myself in some television show. I don't even remember what I was watching, but I sat there in the den and willed the steam off my day. I was desperate to return to calm, to lose myself in some silly reality-type show that might take me from my own reality. Every few moments I'd hear Phil puttering around. He went upstairs—headed probably to Toby's room, or to our home office. He always went up to kiss Toby good night, and tuck her in, even if she was already asleep, so this wasn't unusual. What was unusual, though, was when he came back downstairs and didn't come into the den to discuss what had taken place that afternoon. I had made all these little peace offerings, and he continued to freeze me out. He passed by the den a couple times, and he wouldn't even look at me. Again, this was completely unlike him, to ignore me for such a long stretch, to stay mad. This just wasn't Phil—we would never go to bed angry, even after our toughest battles. He might fall asleep on the couch watching TV, but we'd always talk it out before retiring to the bedroom. It was one of our things.

Later, about ten o'clock or so, I heard him in the bathroom. It sounded like he was getting ready to go to bed. I called out a good night, but once again he didn't say anything, and after that I thought, *Fine, I'll sleep in the den tonight.* Or maybe I thought I'd curl up in the "sleepover" bed in Toby's room. For some reason, I felt like I just couldn't be next to him. It would be the first time during this whole ordeal that we wouldn't sleep in the same bed, but I didn't care. I didn't even care that I was allowing myself to stay angry at a man who couldn't help himself. It was like being mad at a child.

At some point, when I figured Phil was asleep, I pulled myself from the couch in the den and trundled up to Toby's room and got into her extra bed. Later that night, I woke with a start and raced downstairs to check on Phil. It was dark in our bedroom, but there was enough light coming in from the hallway to see that he was under the covers. I took that as a good sign. Some nights, I'd find him asleep on top of the covers, and I'd have to tuck him in, but on this night he had the covers pulled up. I don't remember if I leaned over to give him a kiss before I left the room. I should have. I meant to. But I don't remember.

The next morning, Toby and I were up before the sun, which is how it goes when you have an infant in the house. We were sitting in our screened-in porch, listening to the early morning songbirds. I drank my morning coffee, while Toby sipped her warm morning soy milk. We sat quietly waiting for our day to begin, watching the sun rise. We had some time to fill before waking Daddy, and before getting started on our errands and adventures, so breakfast in the kitchen was next. In the beginning stages of the depression, Phil would drag himself out of bed and push Toby in the jogging stroller before her day of activities. As his doctor had recommended, a workout a day helps keep the doctors away, and he had recently begun including Toby in his exercise routines. Lately, though, he hadn't been working out much at all. Heck, he had trouble even leaving the house!

Finally, we went to wake him up. This, too, was part of our new routine. We'd sing a happy song we had grown used to singing every morning:

> *Good morning to you,*
> *Good morning to you,*
> *We're all in our places.*
> *With bright shiny faces . . .*

We tried to make a singsong, happy time of it, but there were some mornings in there when I caught myself screaming the song more than I was singing it; that's how frustrated I was, how difficult it was to get Phil moving each morning. I'd have Toby on my hip, and she'd be singing, happy as could be, and I'd have to keep myself from reaching for one of the pillows with my free hand and smacking Phil with it, just to get a reaction out of him. And that's how it was on this morning. We sang the song once, and got back nothing. Then we scream-sang the song a second time, and still got back nothing.

Good morning to you,
Good morning to you,
We're all in our places.
With bright shiny faces . . .

Toby was all set to give it a third try when I noticed Phil really wasn't moving. Really, really. I tried to shake him awake, but he was stock-still, so I put Toby down and threw back the covers, and as I did I could see in the corner of my eye a note resting on Phil's nightstand. It could have been anything, that note, but I knew straightaway what it was.

I checked to see if he was breathing, and thanked God that he was. After a beat or two, he seemed to twitch and murmur and try to open his eyes. I grabbed him by the shoulders and began to shake him, like I'd seen people do in the movies. He'd lost so many pounds over the past harrowing months that I was startled by the dead weight of him, and his head lolled about as I shook him. His eyes kept rolling around in his head. I was terrified, and I couldn't think how to help him. It was just a couple seconds, but it felt like forever.

I thought, *Oh my God, Phil, my sweetheart, what did you do?*

Toby was right there with me, so I tried to stay calm. If it had just been me, I would have screamed, but as it was I think I just gasped.

The first thing I did was call my sister-in-law, Liora, who was married to Phil's identical twin brother, Seth. They lived right down the street. "Get over here right now!" I hollered into the phone. I didn't offer up any explanation. There wasn't time—and besides, I'm sure it was a phone call she'd been dreading. Phil had been so out of it, for so long, that we'd all taken turns wondering if his depression might come to something like this.

I hung up the phone, and I remember feeling detached from the situation. I looked at Phil and thought, *I should call 911.* It's like I was inside the moment and removed from it all at the same time. A part of me couldn't grasp that this was actually happening. Time seemed to stand still, and then to hurry up, and then to stand still again.

When the emergency operator picked up, I said, "My husband tried to kill himself. He's barely conscious. I think he took a lot of pills. He left a note. Please hurry."

Then I looked down at Toby, who was just a couple weeks shy of two years old. She was too young to understand what was going on, but I ached for her just the same. I ached for all of us, and in the strange, slow motion of waiting for the ambulance to arrive there was room in my racing imagination for every thought, every prospect, every nightmare scenario. It was all too real, and at the same time it was surreal, like it was a drama unfolding for some other family, and at one point I caught myself reaching to tousle Toby's hair and wanting to tell her that everything was going to be okay, but I couldn't find the words. I'd made those all-important phone calls and then I basically shut down. Nothing made any sense.

I was barefoot, and still in my pajamas, and Liora was over in what seemed forever but was actually a flash, and the police and EMT guys were quickly swarming about the place. I can't remember for certain if Liora got there before the emergency team, or if it was the other way around, but at one point I looked up and noticed someone wheeling a stretcher into the room—into our bedroom!—and it hit me full in the face what we were into. All around, there was this frenzy of activity, and it seemed to me like I was sleepwalking my way through all of it, like it was some sort of bad dream. I remember talking to a whole bunch of different people, but I don't know if I was making any sense. I do know that once Toby was in the living room, away from all the craziness and commotion and walkie-talkies blaring, I finally came back to myself a little bit. I remember feeling dizzy, like I needed to sit down.

Before I left the house, leaving Toby with Liora, I ran into the living room to give Toby a huge hug. I still had no idea what to say to her, but I wanted to tell her everything was going to be okay. I wanted to draw strength from her, if that makes any sense, so I squeezed her tight and held her close and hoped she couldn't see the tears streaming down my cheeks.

Then I raced outside to where they were wheeling Phil into the ambulance, checking his vitals, calling in information on the radio. There was all this haste and heat and activity, and it was all about Phil. All about us. These were our lives, hanging in the balance, and it was too much to take in at just that moment. I didn't know what I was supposed to do, or think. Someone directed me into the front passenger seat of the ambulance, so I shut the door behind me and said, "Let's get going, let's go." I can still hear my voice, all this time later, like I really thought these good, dedicated EMT guys were waiting to move out on my say-so. For some reason, I couldn't stop shaking my head back and forth, like I couldn't believe what was happening and I wanted to chase the reality of it from my thinking. I felt unbelievably fortunate that Phil was still alive, and at the same time furious that he'd done what he'd done. I also felt responsible, in some way, because I knew the tension from the day before had spilled over into his attempt to take his own life. There were all these thoughts bouncing around in my head, and I couldn't keep them straight. All I could think, really, was that we had all suffered enough—even though I knew, deep down, that we weren't done yet.

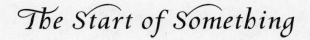

The Start of Something

PHIL

The first sign anything was wrong was in late fall of 2001—and it wasn't exactly a neon sign. There wasn't a parting of the heavens, or a big booming voice, or anything of the kind. Heck, it wasn't even something I paid all that much attention to as it was going on, just a flag I might have seen if I'd known to look for it, something to notice and possibly pay attention to if life wasn't doing its thing to get in the way, if we weren't so busy going through the motions of all those year-end holidays.

Here's something you need to know about Emme and me: we were always big into the holidays, Halloween through Chanukah and Christmas and New Year's. (I'm Jewish; Emme is Christian.) It's just an amazing, special time of year, a chance for family and friends to reconnect and decompress, and in the short time we'd been living in our neighborhood we had become known for our

Halloweens—that, and the kick-butt luge run I built each winter on our back lawn, whenever there was enough snow and freezing temperatures to justify the effort. The funny thing is, we'd moved into our house on Halloween, back in 1997, and over the years we'd marked the calendar with these wonderful celebrations. At some point a few years earlier, we started hanging a sheet in the backyard and showing movies on it, and everybody would dress in costume, the kids and the parents, and we'd have pumpkin painting, apple cider, and hot chocolate for the kids, and beer and wine for the grown-ups, and it was always a great, great time.

This particular Halloween couldn't help but be bittersweet. It was just seven or eight weeks after the September 11 attacks on the United States, and in our little corner of the world in northern New Jersey, just across the George Washington Bridge from Manhattan, folks were still pretty dazed and confused by what was happening downtown, and in the world at large. You have to realize, as suburban New Yorkers, most everyone in our neighborhood knew someone who was killed at the World Trade Center, and in some cases it hit especially close to home. Kids in our community lost parents and aunts and uncles; neighbors lost spouses and siblings; everyone, it seemed, lost a friend— and a sense of innocence we wondered if we'd ever get back. It was a national tragedy played out on our front porch, and we were all a little frayed around the edges, and rubbed raw by the headlines and the terror alerts. And, underneath and alongside everything else, there was the agonizing specter of Ground Zero, which seemed to want to claim our full attention. It was like an open wound that had not yet healed.

And just to add to the bittersweetness of it, there was Toby—our beautiful baby daughter, smiling through her first Halloween without a care in the world but for the smiles she got back in return, from family and friends and good-hearted neighbors looking to catch every possible ray of light in a world that had suddenly grown dark and terrifyingly uncertain. Emme had dressed Toby in an adorable cow outfit, which I guess was some kind of feminist statement, or a nursing mother's subconscious revenge, but it was terrifically cute just the same, and I can remember catching myself a couple times that night, when I wasn't playing host or doling out candy, thinking our lives were about to be jump-started in a big way. We were on the edges of something wonderful and new, and it was about time. Emme and I had been together for a good long while—eleven years!— but we'd gotten around to Toby relatively late in the game. There'd been a couple heartbreaking miscarriages, but we'd waited a long time for Emme's career to really cement itself before we even tried to conceive.

A word or two on Emme's career, which soon after we married became mine as well. Emme was widely known as a plus-size model, although these days the convention is to drop the "plus" and just call her a supermodel. That's fine by me, because she certainly fits that description as well. She modeled clothing and accessories for women who didn't fit the wafer-thin image too often promulgated by movies and fashion magazines and popular magazines— which of course meant that she represented *most* adult

American women (approximately 62 percent), who tend to be a little more full-figured than the models donning the latest line. Along the way, Emme made it her business to promote healthy diet and fitness choices for all women, no matter what their size, and her message took hold in such a way that she soon became a kind of poster girl for a positive body image. She even hosted a show called *Fashion Emergency* on the E! Entertainment Television network, which cast her as a kind of on-call fashion guru for everyday people like you and me, and it got to where she was receiving hundreds of letters and e-mails each week from women who seemed truly grateful to have a "super" role model to call their own.

My job was to work behind the scenes, as husband-turned-manager, and to help promote what we had begun to build, the Emme brand, developing a line of full-figured clothing, coordinating public appearances and speaking engagements, negotiating endorsement deals, and on and on. Just to give you an idea of the far-reaching impact of Emme's positive message, we even launched an "Emme" doll, a collectible, full-figured doll we designed because we thought Barbie needed a curvy friend, and because all school-age girls needed every opportunity to feel good about themselves and their appearance.

Before Toby was born, we were all over the place—traveling on fashion shoots, promoting Emme's latest book, and lecturing to school and community groups across the country. It was a heady, whirlwind existence, and what we loved most of all about it was that we were able to help a whole lot of people along the way. The red-carpet stuff that comes with being married to a supermodel was actually a lot of fun, but that was just a side benefit. The real windfall was that we could wake up each morning and feel good about what we were doing, because thousands upon thousands of women were feeling better about themselves as a result. That and the fact that we got to work side by side left us feeling pretty darn blessed, and now that baby made three we were feeling even more blessed, if such a thing is possible. Sure, Emme had to pull back a bit in the months leading up to Toby's birth, and the plan was for her to take some time off from modeling for the first few months afterward, at least until we could get a handle on this new parenting business.

In any case, there we were, a full-fledged, fully realized family, and like everyone else of our acquaintance our world had been rocked by those terrorist attacks, and what should have been a joyous time in our lives was now tinged with tension and sadness and uncertainty. I looked at my gorgeous wife and our precious baby girl and couldn't shake the thought that everything had just gotten a whole lot more serious and substantial than it had ever been before. Don't get me wrong. I wasn't overwhelmed or disconcerted or tentative about any of this. In fact, my feelings were quite the opposite—and all to the good. There was a wellspring of love and support in our backyard that Halloween night, and I found myself bound up in it and enjoying the ride. I was a father, at long last.

The only real tap on that wellspring was the ongoing ordeal of my younger brother, Jonathan, who had been fighting brain cancer for the previous fifteen years. Talk about bittersweet. It was the underlying sadness of our family, and yet Jonathan was shouldering his illness with tremendous courage and humor, to where we all took turns feeling that he was the one doing the comforting while the rest of us struggled. Man, he was an inspiration! Jonathan's doctors had given him just three to five years, back when he was first diagnosed, and here he was, all this time later, still managing to goad the rest of us into smiling at the absurdity of the human condition, still finding hope and dignity where others might have seen only despair—and even now, as his cancer took yet another turn for the worse, a part of me believed he would beat it back for another fifteen years. It was what he did, and he did it valiantly—although as it turned out he didn't have another fifteen years in him. He would lose his struggle to cancer in January 2004, and with his passing a light seemed to go back on for me, lifting me almost spiritually from my depression.

I'll fill in the details of Jonathan's passing and the ups and (mostly) downs of my depression as we move along in these pages, but it was through Jonathan that I learned there's a black car that pulls up in front of everybody's house at some point. There's no avoiding that black car. It's gonna find you sooner or later. It could be your brother or sister, or your wife, or your parents. It could be you. It could be an unfathomable attack on our American way of life. It could be anything, at any time. The trick, I realized, was in how you deal with whatever bad patches come your way, and in accepting that we all deal with things in our own way, in our own time. And the thing of it is, when we're up against it, we do manage to get on with our lives. We do. We have no choice, I guess.

So there I was, with all of these things going on, all of these emotions rolled up and bundled together, all of these crossroads and milestones intersecting on the wild map of my life—and at some point I caught myself thinking, *Okay, Phil, you're doing okay.* Life, for the most part, was good, and my head was bouncing back and forth between the grim echo of our heightened terror alerts, and the wonder of a new baby daughter, and the worsening of my brother's cancer, but the abiding feeling was one of hope and purpose and good cheer. I was looking ahead, to whatever might come next.

The trouble was, what came next hit me completely unaware. Remember, this was Halloween—October 31, 2001—and by the time I looked up it was mid-November, and I couldn't lift myself out of bed for trying. I didn't see it coming, and I didn't pay all that much attention to it until I was in its middle, but at some point I was overcome by this odd lethargy that was completely out of character for me. It came on gradually at first, left me feeling more and more tired each day, and less and less willing or able to pick myself up and dust myself off and get on with things in anything like my usual way. I had always been this hard-charging, get-it-done type of guy, and yet here I was, feeling suddenly and inexplicably fatigued. All over. All the time. And for no reason I could readily determine. It was the strangest thing, and I didn't know what to make of it. I think it took Emme a couple beats to realize anything was going on beyond a garden-variety virus or bug, and I'm guessing it took me a couple beats longer than that. It's only in retrospect, set against everything that's happened since, that I began to recognize this as the first sign of the depression that would consume me for the next two and a half years.

Here's how it took hold: I developed some sores under my tongue. No big deal, and no doctor has ever drawn a straight line from those sores to the depression that would follow, but this was the sequence. Was there a connection, or some kind of cause and effect? Who can say? All I know is that first there were these sores, and soon after that I couldn't lift my head off the pillow. By the time Thanksgiving rolled around, I wasn't quite myself; I was a little distracted, put off a bit by these sores, wondering if there was something really wrong with me or if it was just a flu-type virus I needed to get past. The sores were a nuisance, nothing more, but soon enough I started to feel tired. Dead tired, all the time, no matter what I'd done during the day or how much sleep I'd had the night before. Getting out of bed became a huge burden. Some days I'd catch myself making these little deals in my own head. *Okay, Phil,* I'd tell myself. *If you get up now, you can still put in a couple hours on the phone making business calls before the day is shot.* Things like that. It was an enveloping malaise, and after a couple weeks the sores were gone, but this all-over fatigue remained.

There was no explaining it. Someone suggested that maybe it was Epstein-Barr, a fairly common virus that can cause mononucleosis and can leave sufferers feeling drained and exhausted—emotionally, physically, and every which way in between. Someone else thought it was an aftershock reaction to the events at the World Trade Center, or maybe a sensory-overload coping mechanism to the latest bad news about my brother Jonathan, or to the pressures of being a new father. For a while, Emme even thought what I was experiencing was some kind of jealous reaction to Toby's birth; Emme's thinking was that I'd been the center of her attention for the longest time, and now we had a daughter who had quite naturally moved front and center in this regard, and I was having a little trouble making the adjustment. I didn't buy that, but I was in no position to argue the point. Whatever it was, I couldn't quite put my finger on it, or get my head all the way around it, but after a couple weeks or so the sores were gone, and I still had to coach myself out of bed each day. I was lethargic, that's the best way to put it, but it was a deep, consuming kind of lethargy, unlike anything I'd ever experienced. I mean, I was square in the middle of what should have been a joyous holiday season, my first Chanukah and Christmas with my baby daughter, a stretch of days I'd been looking forward to on some level my entire life, and I couldn't get myself excited about any of it.

Emme told me later that my eyes had a kind of glassy look to them during those weeks, like I wasn't really there, and when she put it that way it reminded me of how I felt at the time. Like the world was passing me by. Like I couldn't be bothered. Like my life was happening to someone else— or that it was happening to me, but I was too disinterested to take part.

We had an office in our house at the time, and a wonderful assistant who came in to work every day—our dear friend Amy Fierro—and during business hours the house seemed to buzz with haste and purpose and activity, but I managed to tune it all out. Emme, even Amy would keep coming into our room trying to get me out of bed and moving around. Every half hour or so, I'd hear, "Come on, Phil, time to get going." And I'd hear myself pleading for another fifteen minutes of sleep, my voice swallowed up by the pillows, until eventually I'd manage to drag myself out of bed and into the office. I don't know that I accomplished all that much during this strange period, other than dragging myself out of bed, but there it was, and it was all in such marked contrast to how things usually were with me that I almost didn't recognize myself, or the life I was living. Typically, I'd be the one up and out of bed at first light—heading out for an early run, or a bike ride, or a trip to the gym. I was the kind of guy who got more things done in those early-morning hours than most people accomplished in an entire day (hey, I sound like an army recruitment ad!), and all of a sudden it was an effort just to get up each morning.

It wasn't just the mornings that were tough. Some days I'd catch myself zoning out at four or five in the afternoon. I wouldn't have done anything all day long, in terms of physical exertion, and then late in the afternoon I'd start to crash. It was like a giant cloud came over me—or more accurately, like I had these weights on my eyelids, the way they used to draw them on those old Warner Bros. cartoons.

Still, throughout this period, we tried to keep up with the rest of our lives. Yes, it was a consuming thing, but it wasn't an *all*-consuming thing. I was able to take Toby for a walk each day, and return a couple phone calls, and put up a good front. Some mornings I'd even manage a run with Toby in our jogging stroller. I was able to function, running on half empty. That was the key difference from what would happen next. At this point, for this stretch of weeks, I *did* manage to drag myself out of bed each morning, and I *did* manage to keep from shutting down when those weights started to appear on my eyelids, and I *did* go through just enough of my usual motions to leave me thinking I had things under control. Of course, from time to time my fatigue got the better of me. Once, we went to visit some good friends, and I actually fell asleep at the dinner table. Poor Emme was mortified, but at the same time she was dumbfounded and sick with worry. The running joke among our friends, whenever we rent a movie, whether it's an action flick, or a romantic drama, or a comedy, is that I'll be the first one to fall asleep, but this was different. This was me nodding off over dinner (practically in the soup!), during an interesting conversation that at any other time would have left me feeling invigorated.

On another occasion, we were readying the house for one of our trademark holiday parties, and I had the fireplace going, and we'd prepared a sensational meal, and I think I even opened a couple bottles of wine to let them breathe before I went into our bedroom, where Emme was breast-feeding Toby. I took one look at my two girls, and before our first guests even arrived I just lay down on the bed and said, "I could go to sleep right now." And I did.

It was a nagging worry, but I felt like I had a handle on it. I was just a little more tired than usual, that's how I explained it away in my own head, but just to be on the safe side I went to see my cardiologist, Dr. Benjamin Lewis, at New York Presbyterian Hospital–Columbia University Medical Center in Manhattan, more commonly known as Columbia Presbyterian. Here's another relevant piece of personal history: a couple years earlier, I'd developed a condition known as atrial fibrillation, which leaves your heart beating at irregular intervals in such a way that you don't get enough blood flow to the head and your entire system is thrown out of whack. I became aware of it rather suddenly, which is how it often happens. In 1997, we were flying home from Scandinavia after Emme had launched a department store's clothing line there, and my heart started to feel like it was thumping right out of my chest—again, like in one of those old cartoons. For about two or three minutes there, I thought I was going to implode, which I later learned made sense, because my heart was racing at about three hundred beats per minute. This would happen for a period of eight seconds or so. My heart rate returned to normal after just a short while, and the rest of the flight passed without incident, but as soon as I got back to New York I had a thorough checkup, and that's how I wound up in the care of Dr. Lewis, who basically became my general doctor at that point. He put me on beta-blockers, and I got the afib under control, and once I adjusted to the fact that I'd have to take heart medications for the rest of my life, I was back to my old self. Running. Riding my bicycle. Exercising at the gym. Like nothing had happened.

Until now, in the middle of this uncharacteristic malaise, when Dr. Lewis ran some blood tests and determined that the thing to do was to tweak my medications, thinking perhaps that the cocktail of beta-blockers was contributing to this sudden drop in my energy levels—and at some midpoint in the tweaking my fatigue pretty much lifted. Dr. Lewis even encouraged me to see another cardiologist, Dr. James Reiffel, for a second opinion, and they concurred that whatever I was experiencing was most likely *not* heart related. It was the strangest thing, this coming and going of my condition, but whereas at the onset the exhaustion came on somewhat gradually, here it disappeared rather suddenly. There was no explaining it, really. Dr. Lewis didn't think it had anything to do with the new beta-blockers he'd prescribed. In fact, the first new drug he and Dr. Reiffel put me on, flecainide, actually made me feel *more* tired, but I guess it didn't matter. One day I was knocked out and fairly dragging, and the next I was good to go, and I didn't have it in me to question the shift in gears. Over the past few weeks, I'd let things slide in the office, and there was too much work to do—and besides, when you're feeling good and back to yourself, who thinks to question it? So I returned to the rest of my life like nothing had happened, and resolved to make the new year a good one, to make the most of whatever time we had left with Jonathan, and to pour my heart and soul into my family.

And that, for the time being, was that.

As the World Turns

EMME

I can't emphasize how unsettling that holiday season was, how stressful, how not like himself Phil seemed to be. And I'd have to go all the way back to September 2001 to start putting all the pieces back together. I don't know that there's any kind of real connection there for Phil, whether the fatigue he experienced that December had anything at all to do with the 9/11 attacks, but they certainly bathed that entire fall in an unfamiliar light, stretching on into that first chunk of winter. For me, anyway, it's all tied in, and I can't go back and look at one without also thinking about the other.

Also, I believe it's important to place Phil's professional responsibilities into some kind of context. What we do for a living is all wrapped up in who we are and how we live. In Phil's case, he was under a great deal of pressure after Toby was born, and after it had become clear that I could not be out there in the same kind of public way that I had been with frequent client and production dinners, movie premieres and fashion shows. Of course, it was a pressure he put on himself, because my career was taking an interesting new turn, and for a while there it was unclear what role Phil would take in the steering. For one thing, there was Toby. For the first six months of her life, coinciding with those few months that Phil couldn't seem to get jump-started, my wonderful sister, Melanie, helped us out. The plan had been for Phil to be a kind of at-home father, managing Emme Associates from our home office, and taking charge of every visual aspect of the business—from advertising and marketing, in-store displays, direct-mail programs and "brand" identity to custom holiday cards, corporate letterhead and correspondence materials. We thought that would still leave time for him to be the point person if Toby needed anything during the day, to make sure she was safe and happy and well. Meanwhile, I would devote my professional energies to making my new clothing line a success and getting back into the television business. But that plan was obviously scratched when he was in that weird "down" period, so Melanie bailed us out, and when Phil was doing a bit better and it came time for Melanie to move on, I started interviewing babysitters. As Melanie's time with us drew to a close, though, Phil actually took a turn for the worse. It got to where he couldn't even answer e-mails, so getting a babysitter we could trust and who was available to work some uncertain hours was key.

It was a crazy time for us. I had made my name as a model up to this point, and then I had that nice long run as host of *Fashion Emergency,* and had developed a good public persona, but as a nursing mother I really had to pull back for a while and step out of the spotlight. I think I made one television appearance early on, and I had to go through two or three tops because my breast milk kept on coming in so heavy, and I thought, *Screw this! I cannot go on the air right now!* I didn't have the head for it, if that makes any sense, and I certainly wasn't body-ready for it either. Please understand, I don't diet, because I think it wreaks havoc on your body and self-esteem, but I do love to exercise and eat well. Plus, I know my body and my definition of looking good. From a holistic point of view, if I don't feel good about myself, it's impossible to project a positive image through a television camera or a fashion photographer's lens. Still, I knew in time that the weight would come off, so that wasn't the issue. It came down to focus, really, and the fact that my body was not my own, at just that moment. God bless all those models and actresses who are able to give birth and turn up on a red carpet two weeks later, looking fantastic. I don't know what's in their water, but whatever it is it sure wasn't in mine, and I was doing well with that. All I needed, really, was to put my energy into being a mother, and this TV-ready public-appearance stuff just got in the way of that, big time.

We were closing a deal with a company called Kellwood to manufacture a line for JCPenney, and it was all very hectic, and Phil had always been this highly creative person, just brimming with ideas and energy and a unique way of looking at the world. He used to tell people he was the VEO of our company, for visual executive officer, and that was really his strength. That was what he brought to the table. He saw things a little bit differently than anyone else, so he was totally in charge of our "look." Web site design, pictures that had to be approved, promotional materials . . . that was all Phil's vision, and I don't think there was anyone better suited to it. He was a creative soul, and this was where he shined. The straightforward business stuff, negotiating deals, reading over contracts, opening up new opportunities . . . I think he struggled with some of that, to be honest, and if he was being honest he'd say the same. Make no mistake. He was a quick study, and he could hold his own, but I think he worried that he was out of his element, that he wasn't a manager in the traditional sense; and once I got pregnant and it became clear that I was no longer a working model, and once the E! show went into reruns and I committed to being a mom, I think he began to carry this great pressure. I don't know that we ever really talked about it, in just these terms, but our roles were changing and upside down and all over the place, and I think he was left feeling like he had to pull a pie out of the sky for us.

So that was our mind-set, driving downtown on that fateful morning, just as those jet planes crashed into the Twin Towers. We had Toby with us, and we had just crossed the George Washington Bridge and were headed to our showroom at 1411 Broadway, between Thirty-ninth and Fortieth Streets. Just then, as we were inching down Seventh Avenue toward Times Square, nine o'clock or so in the morning, our assistant Amy called us on our cell phone. She was back in our home office in Jersey, and she wanted to know where we were, exactly. I told her we were a couple blocks north of Times Square, a straight shot to the Jumbotron screen that looked to be a mile away.

"Can you see the screen?" she said. "The Times Square screen? From where you are, can you see it?"

I looked ahead, and in the distance saw some bizarre, grainy footage that looked like it had come from some disaster movie. "What is that, *Godzilla*?" I said. I actually said that—probably one of the all-time foolish comments to ever leave my lips!—because that's how it looked, driving down Seventh Avenue, facing up at that giant screen, like a badly made Japanese disaster movie. Like a tiny model plane had bumped into some fake skyscraper. It didn't look real, and even when Amy explained what had happened and what was happening, I still couldn't match what she was saying to what I was seeing on that giant screen.

We managed to make our way to the showroom before the city shut down. That turned out to be a mixed blessing, because once we were there we couldn't leave. The bridges were all closed, and public transportation was for the most part nonexistent, and there wasn't a hotel room to be had on the entire island of Manhattan, so we ended up trudging to stay with our friends Brad and Michelle in their apartment uptown. I remember thinking, *Thank God Toby's with us*—although now, looking back, I realize she would have been better off back home in New Jersey, safely across the river from all this chaos and confusion and the huge, huge mushroom cloud of black soot that seemed to rise from lower Manhattan and roll its way uptown, except for the small detail that I was breast-feeding her at the time. It was all a little too terrifying, too close, too much, and at some point not long after the second tower fell I huddled close with Phil and Toby and wondered how we were going to make it out of the city alive. I was never before as scared as I was at just that moment, in just that time and place. I felt trapped, and I guess I panicked. I went into survival mode, grabbing everything I thought Toby, Phil, and I might need, and yelling for everyone to leave the showroom and get themselves someplace safe.

At one point, I caught myself staring at Phil for the longest time. He was distracted by Toby, and completely unaware that I was staring at him, but it was the kind of moment where you need to pull back and assess. Anyway, that's how it felt to me at the time. We were in the middle of the biggest human catastrophe any of us had ever known, and I had no idea what the rest of the day might bring, so I looked at my husband and tried to soak him in. I thought, *My God, we've come a long way!* And we had. We'd known each other nearly twenty years by this point. We had gone to Syracuse University together, but we hadn't actually met until the last two months of our senior year. We were even in the same school—the School of Visual and Performing Arts—but our paths had never really crossed. It's funny how that works. Even funnier, it was Phil's roommate who hit on me. He sent me a letter, expressing his interest, but I was seeing another guy at the time, so I suggested we all go out as friends—Phil and his roommate, and me and my roommate. And guess what. Phil and I hit it off. We got along great, in a best friends sort of way. We ended up spending parts of every day together, right up until graduation. It was completely platonic. He even ended up sleeping over at my place one night, because he was too drunk or too tired to go back home, and before he got into bed I said, "Okay, Phil, there's a line that runs right down the middle of this bed. Keep your underwear on and keep to your side of the bed."

We kind of drifted apart after graduation. I went off to Los Angeles and worked as a page at NBC, while Phil took this really great gig playing guitar and singing with his brother Seth at all these different Club Med resorts throughout the Caribbean. From L.A. I moved to Arizona and worked for a while as a television news reporter, and eventually I drifted back to New York and figured I'd look up my old friend. Phil had moved back to New York as well, and was working with his dad and brother in a family advertising agency. We picked up right where we left off. I was still seeing that same someone else at the time, although that relationship was on its last legs, and Phil was on again, off again with a someone else of his own, but we started hanging out, just like back in college. Until one night, when Phil showed up at my fourth-floor walk-up on East Sixty-fifth Street wearing a clown nose and holding a dozen roses to take me to some black-tie Junior League event. It cracked me up—but then Phil was always cracking me up. He said, "I have a feeling this party might be a little stuffy."

He was right; it was.

That was a turning-point night for us, because Phil dragged me onto the dance floor and started strutting to some Earth, Wind & Fire and managed to *turn* his ankle. (Get it? A turning point? That's the kind of corny joke my husband would tell, so I guess his sense of humor has rubbed off on me.) Anyway, he really did a job on himself, and I took one look at the ankle and knew he needed to ice it. We ended up going back to my place, and talking all night long, and once again Phil needed to stay over because he couldn't drive his stick-shift Jeep with his ankle so swollen, only this time there wasn't exactly a line running down the middle of the bed, if you get my drift.

Okay, so that's the story of how we met. And here we were, all these years later, trying to make sense of our world in the middle of the chaotic streets of Manhattan, and trying to outrun this ominous black cloud of soot, with our infant daughter in tow. I caught myself thinking back to our marriage vows, specifically to the *for better or worse* part, and I realized that this is what people mean when they talk about the worst of what life has in store.

That black cloud hung over New York City for weeks—in a literal sense, but in a figurative one as well. There were even a couple mornings in the days that followed when the ash would reach across the Hudson to New Jersey, and the acrid smell of smoke was thick and all around, but what lingered long after the smoke and ash had cleared was the sense that we were no longer safe, and that our futures were no longer certain, and that our legs could be pulled out from under us at any time. What should have been a happy, blessed time in our lives—a season of firsts for little Toby, who was born on August 10, 2001—was now stained by this one black day. It's like something was taken from us, and I don't mean to come across as self-absorbed or anything, because God knows friends and neighbors lost a whole lot more than we did in these attacks, but that's how it left me feeling.

What people around the country don't realize is how

close to home and in your face those attacks were to those of us in the New York City area, and when I think back to the Halloween night that Phil wrote about in the previous chapter, I remember how hesitant everyone was that year to even let their kids out of the house to go trick-or-treating in their own neighborhood; once we were all together and celebrating, it's like we were all feeling guilty, a little bit, for losing ourselves in something simple and silly like a Halloween party so soon after such a terrible tragedy. It's like we didn't deserve even this small piece of happiness, and underneath that guilt was a mounting sense of insecurity, like we were all waiting for some other shoe to drop, for the next monstrously bad thing to happen, and I have to think that all of these emotions had something to do with the funk Phil found himself in that December. As we've learned in all the research we've done since Phil's depression, and all the conversations we've had with other couples who've gone through something similar, it's never just one thing.

Sometimes, it seemed that black cloud was ours alone. It was weird. From time to time I'd catch myself thinking we were headed for some major stuff, like we'd dodged some sort of bullet but that there was another bullet out there with our name on it. They were just passing thoughts, and when I talk to my girlfriends I sense that a lot of new mothers have them, and I don't mean to place too much emphasis on those thoughts—but there they were. There was one afternoon in particular, when I was sitting on the edge of our bed and the house was fairly quiet. Toby was napping. Phil was out and about. Amy was in the office, but I was lost in my thoughts, and as it happened they ran to

Phil. I don't think his sudden exhaustion had set in just yet, his shutting down early, but I guess I could feel it coming because I caught myself thinking, *Okay, Emme, there's something going on with Phil. He's about to go off on a journey that's going to be very difficult, very trying, but he'll be okay. We'll all be okay.* It was a very nonspecific thought, and it could have meant anything or nothing at all, and I realize that it's only in hindsight that it looms as some sort of sign of what was about to happen. It's a terrifying thing, to think the very worst might happen to someone you love, and once the first thought hit I couldn't shake all these related thoughts that passed through my head, thoughts about what life would be like without Phil, how Toby and I would handle such a loss, and on and on. Like I said, it was terrifying, but at the same time it was also comforting. I was overcome with a sense that, whatever was about to happen, it would shake out okay. We'd get past it, and we'd be stronger and better and closer for having done so.

Pretty creepy, right? Our boat was about to be rocked big time, I felt sure of it, but I had no idea how, or when, or why. All I could do was wait for it, and ride it out, and know that we'd be okay on the other side of it. Depression? If you'd have asked me at the time, I'd have said you were crazy, but I guess in the back of my mind I somehow knew. I saw all these subtle, inconspicuous changes happening in Phil, and set them against the major changes happening in the world around us, and I just knew. Deep down. And when Phil's depression finally did creep in, we were all in quicksand, and as we struggled to climb out of it I drew comfort from this earlier "vision."

But it wasn't just the all-over fatigue we should have seen as a sign; Phil had become a little short-tempered as well. This, too, was completely uncharacteristic, but at the time I guess I thought he was tired, and lackluster, and on edge, and I explained away this shift in personality as having to do with his general weariness. He wasn't himself, that's all it was. He was shutting down earlier and earlier each day. There was a lot on his mind. He was worried about Jonathan, and stressed about the business.

One incident stands out. We were sitting in the den one night that December, and I was breast-feeding Toby, and Phil and I started to argue. I no longer recall what the argument was about, but after we had both seemed to have had enough of it, I said, "Look, Phil, can we talk about this later? Please, I'm breast-feeding. I really want to be calm right now." There was a lot going on, and Jonathan wasn't doing all that well, and Phil was tired and out of sorts, and I thought we could just put a pin in whatever it was we couldn't agree on and deal with it later.

Well, you'd have thought I'd asked Phil to rob a bank, from the way he reacted. He screamed—also, completely *not* like him!—and then he threw a pillow across the room to where I was sitting, and demanded that I hand Toby over to him, immediately. It was the most incongruous thing, coming from my gentle soul of a husband. Really, it wasn't him at all. He made like he wanted to storm out the door, and take Toby with him.

"I don't love you anymore!" he shouted, and the words just kind of hung there between us, and I didn't know what to make of them, because they came out of nowhere. I took a deep breath and encouraged Phil to go outside and cool off, and once he was gone I thought, *Okay, Emme, now what the hell was that all about?* Really, it was the most peculiar thing, and so far off the map of how he usually was and how we were as a couple and as friends. I knew in my heart how he truly felt, so I just chalked it up to stress and didn't go down that road. I was in a kind of shock, but I wasn't mad, and I wasn't frightened. I was confused, but then I convinced myself that this was just Phil, with a short fuse and running on fumes, probably as a result of everything else that was going on in our lives.

He came back a short while later, and he was calm, so we put it behind us and moved on, and by the next morning, it was like it hadn't even happened. We didn't talk about it, because there was a whole mess of new stuff to worry about by that point, like getting Phil up and out of bed, and dealing with whatever was going on with work, and the increasingly apparent problem that we didn't have a good infrastructure in place with the business to absorb my not being around as much because of Toby. And yet during all of this craziness I still don't think it occurred to either one of us that we were dealing with a depression. Whatever it was, whatever we wanted to call it, we pretty much forgot about it for the time being and went back to our routines.

In all, Phil's fatigue lasted for about four or five weeks, and it left him as quickly as it came on. There was a point of pause in there, in March 2002, when Phil and Seth disappeared for a few days to St. Maarten with Jonathan, for a kind of last-chance getaway while Jonathan was still feeling well enough to travel. Jonathan's doctors had just told him his condition had gotten worse and that he probably had another six to twelve months to live, so his brothers arranged for this last-hurrah-type vacation. Phil came back and told me this heartbreakingly funny story about how the three of them had gone for a walk on the beach one morning, with Jonathan in the middle, and Phil and Seth had gotten into some intense conversation about something or other, and all of a sudden they looked around and there was no one in the middle. They'd just been walking, and talking, and laughing, and they turned around to see Jonathan, about twenty or thirty feet back, flailing in the sand, having some kind of seizure. They raced to his side, and jumped on him, and held down his arms and legs until the seizure passed, and when it did they all had a good laugh about it, because it was so damn sad that it struck them as hilarious.

The great thing about that trip to St. Maarten, though, other than the fact that Phil and his brothers had managed to carve out this special pocket of time for each other, was that Phil seemed to have really gotten past his December funk. For a while he was back to his old self—happy, involved, and good as new. Sure, he was weighed down some by the onrushing sorrow of the prospect of losing Jonathan, but the counterweight to that unhappiness was the lift he got from Toby, the gift it felt like he was unwrapping every time he got out of bed. It's like his entire outlook changed, and I thought back to that weird *what if?* The thought I'd had that one afternoon on the edge of my bed. I hoped against hope that this had been his difficult journey, and that it was all the way behind us.

Over the next weeks and months, I did notice Phil spending more and more time with Toby, which I thought was wonderful. He had all his energy back, and a little bit more besides, and he was eager to greet each new day like it had some wonderful surprises in store. He was just so psyched to go to work each morning, whether it was to the showroom to check on the latest graphic designs for the Emme Collection, or to take a meeting in Manhattan about some new project or other, or to spend some time answering the e-mails that needed attention. Even more than the work, he was psyched to get back to his old routine of taking Toby in the jogging stroller when he went out on his run each morning. He was such a tremendous father, like I always knew he would be—dancing with her, pushing her on the swings. In the morning, he'd bring her in to bed with me and we'd lay there, the three of us, basking in the warm light of family and spring and hopefulness and all those good things, and it was during these moments when Phil's brief bout with exhaustion and his outbursts of temper seemed like they had happened in some other time, because all was once again right in our little world.

My Chronic Pain

I had such a blast in St. Maarten with Seth and Jonathan that I convinced Emme to take a short getaway there, just the two of us. It was April 2002, and we hadn't been away together since Toby was born eight months earlier, and with everything I'd put Emme through that winter I wanted the chance to make it up to her, so I cleared our schedule and made all the arrangements. I even booked the same hotel where I had just stayed, because it was such a nice place, and the entire time I was there with my brothers I kept thinking it would be the perfect spot for a romantic weekend.

And it was. For three or four days, we managed to put all the tension of those months behind us. We lay in the sun. We swam. We drank. We ran. We danced. We laughed. This last was key, because we realized we hadn't laughed in the longest time—not together, anyway, not really. The truth is, there hadn't been much to laugh about. Sure, there was the constant joy of Toby, who offered every reason to smile, but underneath there had been the harrowing threat to U.S. security, the latest bad news about Jonathan's cancer, the disquiet of my months-long funk, and the confusion over what Emme described as my short temper. To tell the truth, I didn't even remember flying off the handle those few times, when apparently I'd said some hurtful things, but that was all behind us now, and I was back to myself, and we had only to soak in those rich Caribbean sunsets to know that our world could be a charmed and wondrous place. The black clouds that briefly cast a pall over our days had finally lifted.

We returned to New Jersey refreshed and recharged, and I jumped right back into my work with Emme Associates, ramping up for the launch of our new clothing line, reviewing new business opportunities, meeting with our William Morris agents, and expanding the Emme brand in exciting new ways. That was to be our focus in the weeks ahead: working out a major next move for when Emme was ready to return to the public eye, for when Toby was just a little bit older. My head had been all over the place the past few months, and it was an exhilarating thing to rediscover my focus, to get back up to speed and await the next challenge.

Whenever possible, I stole away some precious time with Toby, sneaking out of the office when things were slow to take her for a walk, or to read to her, or just to horse around on our living room floor. When the weather was nice I'd take Toby out for a good long run, and I'd lose myself in the rhythm of those soft footfalls against pavement and think there was no place in the world I'd rather be, nothing else I'd rather be doing than running free with Toby in tow—or, I should say, with Toby in *push*. It was such an idyllic time in our lives, at least for a few weeks there, especially in contrast to the bleakness of the previous few months. I could have gone on like that forever. Toby was such an expressive, joyful little soul that I used to think how great it would be if I could just put things on freeze-frame and keep her at that age forever. Of course, parents of little kids are always saying that whatever age their kid happens to be at a particular moment is the *best* age, so I'm no different— except for the fact that I missed out on a significant chunk of Toby's first few months, so I tended to place a special emphasis on each new stage in her development.

In any case, there I was, back at it, enjoying life once again, working out, feeling great, being a dad, until one morning, in mid-April or so, when I felt a peculiar sensation while I was trying to urinate. I first felt this peculiar sensation a week or so before Emme and I took off for St. Maarten, and it wasn't all that big a deal at the outset. It wasn't anything, really. It wasn't killer painful or anything like that, not right away. It wasn't even what I would describe as a burning sensation, although that would come soon enough. It was annoying, more than anything else. Noticeable. The best way to describe it is that something felt *off* at the tip of my penis—so much so that I mentioned it to Emme as soon as I got out of the shower that morning.

Forgive me, but you have to realize how difficult it is to write the phrase "at the tip of my penis" with a straight face. I'm a big old adolescent at heart, and I can't keep from snickering. I know, it's silly and unbelievably immature, but that's me. I'm sorry, but even after everything I've been through, I have to laugh. It's embarrassing. And I wish like hell I could be writing about some other part of my body, but this is how it happened, so let me just get the giggles out of my system in this paragraph (and, who knows, maybe out of yours as well), and then I'll get all serious and clinical. I promise.

Another thing worth mentioning to put this first symptom into context is that Emme has a weakness for bathroom products—gels, oils, creams, conditioners, exfoliating kits, mud baths and I don't know what else. All I know is that they all smell good and promise to make my skin or my hair do this or that, so I've tried them all. They're spread out all over our bathroom shower, so how can I not try them? And in our guest bathroom, or the outdoor shower at the beach? Well, you can just about forget it there; Emme's got it set up so that overnight visitors must feel like they've died and gone to a four-star hotel in bath products heaven. Some of the stuff she gets for free, for an endorsement; some of it she collects in goodie bags at fashion shows and other industry events; but most of it she just buys herself, whenever something strikes her as worth trying. It's like a sample sale in our shower, and a grove of citrus smells, which means of course that there's always something new for me to rub on my body, and when I first felt this discomfort I thought maybe I'd inadvertently rubbed some exfoliating stuff where I shouldn't have. Anyway, that was my initial thought. I even called out to Emme from the bathroom, wondering if it was possible to get a piece of exfoliant caught at the end of your penis. She allowed, quite reasonably, that she'd never had that problem, but figured anything was possible.

Still, it was just an irritating thing when I first noticed it, but after we returned from St. Maarten it started to get worse, and I worried that maybe I'd picked up some kind of infection down there, or gotten a particle of sand trapped in my urethra, or some sort of bite while swimming in the Caribbean, so I added these to my checklist of worries and made an appointment to see a doctor before the discomfort got any worse. If there was anything I'd learned from all those years watching my mother manage Jonathan's care, it was to get a head start on even the slightest concern before it got away from you. *See a problem, see a doctor, see it through* . . . these seemed to be the marching orders in my family, so I determined to take a proactive approach. Trouble was, I didn't know where to turn to find a doctor who specialized in this type of case, and no one I knew had ever experienced anything like what I was going through, so it was a crapshoot. I think I ended up going to every urologist on my insurance plan, that's how desperate the situation ultimately became—and how difficult it was for some of these doctors to figure out what was going on. It was just a vague type of penile pain, and no one knew quite what to make of it. In fact, the first doctor I consulted didn't have the first idea what was causing the symptoms, except he was able to assure me that whatever it was had nothing to do with Emme's exfoliant or the water in St. Maarten, but meanwhile the discomfort got worse and worse—and, as it did, I naturally became more and more concerned.

Okay, I thought, as I went through these various consultations. *Everybody seems to know what this isn't, but what the hell is it?*

Over the next few weeks, the discomfort went from a weird, ticklish sensation when I peed to an actual burning sensation, and every day the heat seemed to turn up a notch or two on the burning to where soon after that it was unbearable, and soon after that it was fairly constant. It wasn't just when I urinated. The peeing made it worse—exponentially worse—but there was some level of serious pain all the time, and there was nothing I could do to bring any kind of relief. I went to four or five doctors fairly early on, and no one could tell me for certain what was going on down there. It was the most maddening experience, because the pain was excruciating, and the focus was on trying to determine the cause rather than on managing the pain. The idea was that you shouldn't really mask the pain until you knew what was causing it, but the pain was killing me and there was no end in sight. One doctor put me on an eighteen-day course of antibiotics, to treat what he assumed to be an infection in the penile area, but that didn't do anything to address the constant burning; and it turned out not to be an infection that we could just knock out of my system, and at the end of those eighteen days, I was no better off than I had been going in. Another doctor thought it was cystitis, and he put me on a medication called Elmiron, which was meant to coat the urethra in such a way that the burning might ease, but the drug brought no relief and my condition worsened, and at this point when I went to the bathroom it felt like I was peeing razor blades.

That's one thing I'd do differently if, God forbid, I ever find myself experiencing that kind of chronic pain in the future. I'd worry about pain management first, even if a diagnosis wasn't forthcoming, because once the pain starts to get away from you it spirals out of control. That was how it happened for me, it spiraled, and it went from being like a 4 or 5 on a scale of 1 to 10 to like an 8 or 9, and I wished like hell someone had thought to load me up on codeine to deaden the pain. It was a crippling kind of pain. It got to where I couldn't sleep without taking Ambien or some other drug to knock me out. And even when I did manage to find sleep, I was up five or six times a night to go to the bathroom, which was its own double whammy, because each time I urinated, it felt like I would bust out of my skin, and at that point I'd be fully awake and so stressed out by the pain that I would have trouble falling back to sleep.

I couldn't concentrate on any work-related stuff. I couldn't be there for Jonathan. I couldn't give Toby my full attention. I couldn't do a thing but try to cope with the intense pain—and, let me tell you, I wasn't doing such a great job of *that*. We've all heard people talk about a consuming pain, and I guess that's what this was for me. Consuming. Enveloping. Debilitating. It's all I thought about, all I talked about. It's like it ate up everything about me, including my enthusiasm and good cheer and zest for living, and all I could do was wait for it to spit those parts of me back out again so I could get back to living my life.

The closest thing we got to a diagnosis was that I was suffering from something called pelvic pain syndrome, and it was months in coming. I'd never heard of pelvic pain syndrome, but one of these doctors described it for me, and told me I had a lower pelvic floor muscle that wasn't functioning the way it was supposed to. It made no sense to me, but that's what he said, and yet even with that dubious diagnosis there was no medication or treatment he could prescribe to ease my suffering. I thought, *What the hell's the point in giving it a name if there's no way to treat it?* Really, it was like someone had taken a Bunsen burner to my crotch and flipped the burner to high, and no one could offer any relief.

I tried anything and everything. I went to an infectious disease specialist, who put me on a course of doxycycline, with no real relief. I submitted to biofeedback treatments at Columbia Urological Center, which seemed to make things worse. I consulted an NYU urologist who did a urine culture and a urethral culture, but the results came back negative. Another urologist performed a digital rectal exam, which was about as pleasant as it sounds, and proved only that there was nothing urologically wrong with me and that I had developed an even higher threshold for pain than I had once thought. I saw a holistic-type healer known as a medical intuitive, who also happened to be an acupuncturist, and for about fifteen minutes on that table I finally had some relief. There were all these needles in my body, and I looked like a porcupine, but the pain was miraculously gone—even if it was only while the needles were in me; I'd have had to lie on that examination table with needles in me 24/7 if I wanted any type of lasting relief. Still, I took four or five acupuncture treatments, and found myself looking forward to them for the brief respite they offered, but there was no long-term benefit that I could determine.

Next, I was referred to a nutritionist/iridologist who "read" my eyes and determined what type of diet I should be on to ease the pain. She had me taking chlorophyll, coral calcium, flaxseed oil, omega-3 and a lot of other herbs and vitamins that were purportedly high in alkaline content to help relieve the burning sensation. It didn't do much to ease the pain, but I did lose a lot of weight on her treatment program—a side effect I could have done without. On her program, I was *juicing* every morning: kale, carrots, cucumber, wheat grass, celery, spinach, and a little apple to sweeten the mixture.

I even went to a physiotherapist, who was a little outside the box, to say the least. He had me memorizing affirmations, like "I am a child of the universe." Or "I love myself." Or "I can do no wrong." I was supposed to recite these mantras out loud, like a chant, while tapping my wrist with the fingers from my other hand. This guy gave me a tape and a workbook so I could practice this stuff at home, and I made a real effort to follow his plan, but at some point it was just too weird. Plus, on my second and third visits, he began to dismiss or discredit some of the other treatments I'd been receiving, suggesting that he offered the only path to wellness. By this point, I had started seeing a psychiatrist, Dr. Ralph Wharton, who had treated Seth during his depression all those years earlier, and who had lately been offering counsel to my entire family to help us cope with Jonathan's illness. Dr. Wharton had prescribed Xanax for my anxiety, and when the nut-job physiotherapist heard about this, he said, "Phil, if you think a little Xanax is going to help, you are quite mistaken."

I was willing to try anything to alleviate the pain, which had blossomed into an aggressive burning through the shaft and head of the penis and a powerful ache in my prostate area; the only time I was without pain was during the few hours of fitful sleep I managed each night—and, once summer approached and we started heading down to the Jersey Shore to the house we rented on Long Beach Island, where I sat in the cold ocean water. We'd have friends come down to visit, to spend the day on the beach, but I'd pass most of the time in the ocean, freezing my nuts off, deadening the pain. My entire lower region was on fire, and that's what you do to put out a fire, you douse it with water. I didn't care about being a good host to our guests; I was desperate. This became a habit for me, through the July Fourth weekend, when our house rental ran out, and then on and off throughout the summer whenever we would return to the beach for a respite.

Some weeks later, when I was still trying to numb myself in the freezing waters of the Atlantic, I caught myself praying for a riptide to come along and whisk me out to sea, to put an end to the constant pain. Best I can recall, these were the first "suicidal" thoughts I entertained— although, to put a fine point on things, I don't know that they were *really* suicidal, and I certainly wasn't entertained. You know how you're always getting these weird mental pictures and runaway thoughts? How an image alights in your head and you have to shake it clear? That's closer to what was going on here, with these riptide thoughts. I wasn't *longing* for the tides to sweep me out to sea, and I wasn't actively seeking them out; I certainly didn't want to die by drowning, which struck me then and now as a horrible way to go, but there was something calming about the thought of being taken away from all this misery.

The journal I kept sporadically during this period gives a little more insight into what was going on with me:

Aug. 11, '02
Toby had her 1st B-Day! Emme and I shared it with her at LBI. The beach is so awesome! Still not feeling well. My lower region is on fire. I've been trying to heal whatever has been eating at me. . . . Each day has been a major task to live. It sucks being ill. I'm existing, not living! I'm angry, pissed, but most of all weak. I'm physically spent! Toby has helped me by her mere existence. She keeps me going. Emme and Toby are my life. I need to forge forward. Tomorrow I'll see yet another doctor and try to figure out what is wrong with me. I am in constant pain. It's been 3 months of pain. I must release it. I need to live again.

Toby's birthday was a little on the pathetic side, I'm sad to report. It was just the three of us, and a stack of store-bought doughnuts with a candle slapped on top. Of course, little Toby was just a toddler, and had no idea that we didn't have the energy for cake and ice cream and friends and family. She didn't know that anything was missing from her celebration. She was just happy with the clapping and singing and hugging. But I remember feeling awful, like it was my fault, like this was a telling sign of how useless I'd become to my family, how out of it I was. I was such a drain that all I could manage was a stack of doughnuts for my daughter's first birthday party.

I was of no use to Emme at all during that summer. If we entertained friends at the beach, she was on her own. I couldn't even keep up my end of a conversation—that's how intensely focused I was on dealing with the pain. And I was of no use to her in any kind of intimate way, because *that* was just about the furthest thing from my mind. Problem was, it wasn't the furthest thing from Emme's mind. That was one of the things that had always been so great about our relationship, how we both enjoyed each other physically. Back when I was healthy, when Emme was enjoying her first rush of fame, interviewers would always ask me what it was like to be married to a woman who was actually bigger than me. (The joke in our house was that Emme could beat the crap out of me. Only it wasn't a joke—she could!) My pat answer was that it was great. There was more of her to love, I used to say. We had a very healthy sexual relationship, and here I was, for the first time since we'd been together, completely checked out of that healthy sexual relationship, which of course could not have been easy on Emme. I couldn't even talk about it with her; that's how far removed it was from my thinking. Like I said, I was of no use to her in this department.

I was of no use to Toby, either. Whatever momentum I'd recovered after my winter doldrums was now lost to me, and I could barely concentrate on reading to my daughter from one of her little picture books before bedtime. I'd gone from being a great father to being no father at all, back to being a great father, and back again to being no father at all—all in the space of her first year.

We'd been renting that house on Long Beach Island for the previous five summers, and for us, it had always been about peace and solitude. The house belonged to a wonderful family, the McShanes; over the years, they'd become great friends, and they often invited us down for extended visits after our rental period passed. They kept a framed message right over the dining room table—"A waterfront view is not about life or death. It's much more important than that"—and I remember looking at that sign and failing to see the humor in it. When I was well, it struck me as an absurd truth, but when I suffered, throughout the summer of 2002, I just didn't get it.

I didn't get any of the joy and wonder and human comedy that came our way that awful summer. There was one incident that stands out in memory as emblematic of our struggles. Emme was packing up all of our stuff at the end of our rental period. I couldn't do anything to help, because I was too far gone to the pain. When the car was all packed, Emme tackled the fridge. Among the perishables she had to clear out was a container of herring that my mother had brought us when she came to visit, so Emme dumped what was left of it into the garbage disposal and flipped the switch. Well, the disposal turned on and churned the fish, and then all of a sudden a pipe burst and there was fish mash flying all over the place—out the open window just over the kitchen sink and into the open window of our car, which was parked just below. It looked like a whale had thrown up in our car. God, it was disgusting. At any other time in our lives, this would have been the funniest scene, like something out of a Woody Allen movie, but just then it struck poor Emme as a telling and frustrating reminder of what our lives had become—whale spew—while it struck me as another in a long list of distractions that did nothing to take me away from the chronic pain.

The only thing that mattered to me during those horrible weeks was being pain-free, and it was forever just out of reach, and I was slipping deeper and deeper into something I had no control over. That's the scary part of depression. It creeps up on you without announcing itself. You don't recognize it at first, even if you're looking for it, and it's not until it becomes you and you become it that the picture becomes clear.

Back home, my stomach was having a hard time adjusting to the antibiotics my first few doctors had me on to knock out whatever infection they thought might be causing the penile pain. I was on a course of Levaquin for fifteen days, and a course of Ciprofloxacin for another fifteen days, and all I got out of each was a terrible case of constipation. Then I'd take acidophilus and bifidophilus to balance the level of bacteria in my system. I was like a walking chemistry experiment! There were times when I would sit in the bathroom for over an hour, and I still wouldn't be able to go. When I did finally manage a bowel movement, it was a whole other ordeal, and I began to think I had some idea what a woman might go through in childbirth. I'd get off the toilet after all that time and there'd be a nice *queg ring* pressed into my butt—that's the impression the seat leaves on your ass when you've been sitting for too long, and I wasn't so far gone that I couldn't laugh at the sight of it in the mirror. (See, I told you I could be horribly immature! Even in times of great distress!)

Back to that chemistry experiment: my ever-growing team of doctors put together a treatment plan to help me cope with the pain that looked like it might put my medical insurance company out of business. Among the many medications and supplements I took on a daily basis that summer were Sectral, for my atrial fibrillation; coated aspirin, for my afib; Lipitor, for my cholesterol; Vioxx, an anti-inflammatory that has since been taken off the market because it was determined that patients could be at risk for heart attack if they took it for any length of time; vitamin E and multivitamin tablets, for my afib; Tylenol III with codeine; water with chlorophyll; aloe vera juice; pygeum and saw palmetto; acidophilus and bifidophilus—all of it washed down with at least two liters of water per day. Beginning in August, when the depression finally made itself known, I was given an antidepressant called Elavil, and soon after that a Darvon compound and a drug called alprazolam, more commonly known as Xanax.

Looking back, I'd say the signs of depression were evident in the very early part of that summer, but we didn't recognize them as such for a couple more weeks. As time went on, I began to experience some of that same lethargy that had hit me the previous winter—and here I thought it had to do with all the sleep I was losing to this constant pain. There was a clear cause and effect, the way I saw it. I didn't know just then to think in terms of a depression, even though Seth had experienced a depression in his early twenties. (More on this a bit later on.) It was on the map of our shared experience, but it didn't occur to me at the time. Emme says now that she had some idea, by late June or July, that this was where I was headed. She begged me to see a psychiatrist, to at least consult with Dr. Wharton after one of our family sessions to discuss Jonathan, but I kept insisting that I didn't need a therapist. All I needed was to understand and manage and hopefully ease the pain.

I craved sleep, because that was the only way I could be sure to get any kind of relief, but the truth was I didn't sleep all that much. I couldn't. I tossed about, and I longed for it, but it only came in bits and pieces. The medication that was meant to help me sleep mainly left me feeling drowsy and out of it and hoping like hell that I could drift off, even if it was only for a few minutes, but it didn't knock me out and down for the count, which was what I very much needed.

Another journal entry:

Sept. 2, '02
Feeling very down. Pain still exists and is definitely the major reason why I'm depressed. I admit it! Not ashamed of it. I am depressed! It sucks!!! I now can relate to those I know who have battled depression. Man, can't explain it. I'm a bit of a roller coaster, up and down . . . I hope I can make it. The urologist told me that I'll be fine and whatever it is will burn itself out . . . my body seems to be fighting itself. It's a big fucking mind and body battle. I'm seeking spiritual guidance, but it's tough. I ask God for help and I know there is a lesson behind this. I just wish it would be over so I can live

again . . . I'm having problems helping myself! I'm exhausted. I'm weak—great, keep up the negative-speak, asshole!

I couldn't stand the pain. Man oh man, it was just awful, and I don't think I was the best patient in the world. In fact, I'm sure I wasn't. I complained a lot. I don't know that I was eating properly. Also, I'd been avoiding peeing, because it was so excruciating, which meant I wasn't taking in enough fluids, which in the heat of summer meant I was probably dehydrated. (This despite that prescription from the nutritionist to drink at least two liters of water each day!) And sex remained out of the question. It hurt too much to ejaculate, but the doctor stressed that it was important for me to flush out my system and to keep properly hydrated and to try to ejaculate from time to time. Emme wanted to help me out in this area, but I was in agony. I just couldn't do it.

The pain was at its worst as Labor Day approached, although by the end of the year it began to improve—slowly at first, but soon enough to where I wasn't dreading going to the bathroom, or longing for sleep the way I'd been just a few weeks before. The pain was still very much a part of my day-to-day life, but it began to abate somewhat to where I felt I finally had a handle on it. There was reason to hope.

When all was said and done, the chronic pain lasted about eight or nine months, and I was in full-blown agony for six or seven of those months, and by the end I was so beaten down by the ordeal that I couldn't help but be depressed. Also, one of the many monkey wrenches that found me during this time was a killer migraine that somehow clawed its way through all those medications. Emme saw me writhing and suffering and thought I was having some sort of seizure, so she called Dr. Wharton, and he coached us through it. Emme told me later she was putting cold compresses on my head, and massaging my feet to give me some relief, but I don't have any memory of anything but the monster agony of the migraine. It came on quickly, and stayed for a couple hours. Silence and darkness were the only things that seemed to help, and when the migraine finally lifted I was able to sleep, which now killed two birds with one stone, taking me past the chronic pain and the migraine both.

At around this time, everyone around me realized I had undergone some sort of emotional shift. I was *down* all the time, even when the pain became manageable. This was about where I began to think in terms of a depression. I was deep into that same funk mode I'd been in over the previous winter, and I started to have some real trouble getting out of bed each morning, and I was less and less interested in being around other people. The shift didn't exactly happen overnight, but it was fairly sudden, as Emme recalls. Me, I don't really remember, because I guess I was too focused on dealing with the chronic pain. As far as the pain was concerned, on that same scale of 1 to 10, it slipped back down to about a 6 or 7. My "levels" became a constant topic of conversation. It was how Emme and I communicated with each other, and it became a shorthand for how I was doing. One of the keys to my treatment, as I began seeing more and more doctors, and taking more and more medications, was determining my pain and mood thresholds, and to track my ever-changing cocktail of meds against my ever-shifting levels, so Emme was forever asking me, "Where are you?" Meaning, where was the pain and where was my mood . . . all in relation to where they were the day before. Everything was relative.

Were it not for the depression, I could function, at that 6 or 7 pain level. I could sit at my desk and try to pay bills for a short stretch of time, or answer e-mails, or take Toby out for a run. Emme even tried to slot in some social engagements once we got back from the beach, hoping to give us an opportunity to reconnect with friends, but I was hardly able to go through the motions and keep up appearances. If you'd have asked me later what we talked about over dinner, there's no way I could have told you, but at least I showed up.

Exercise was important, Dr. Wharton kept telling me, and a part of me was determined to follow his orders, but another part was unable to do much of anything. All summer long I'd been pretty much a couch potato—or, I should say, a bed potato, or a shoreline potato, because that's where I spent most of my time, trying incessantly to fall asleep or to soak my crotch in the cold waters of the Atlantic Ocean. So I tried to exercise, to get my endorphins going, to muscle my way past the pain.

Anyway, I meant to, but I couldn't get out of my own way for trying. There was a line from some years-ago commercial that kept bouncing around in my head during this period—"my get up and go must have got up and went"—and that pretty much described my mood and my energy levels. (I know, I know . . . it's also a line from a classic Aerosmith song, but I'm pretty sure those guys borrowed it from the commercial.) I knew what was best for me, what I needed to do, what everyone else expected of me . . . but nothing could get me jump-started.

Oct. 15, '02
Never thought I'd get through the morning . . . I can't give in although this is the most difficult race I've ever run. Sometimes I just want to lie down and call it quits. I'm not a quitter but the pain has to stop. I'm very impatient. I want a quick fix but life is not that way. My brain wanders to very dark places. I'm fighting it, but it takes over. I need to live. I have a wonderful life but there are moments I just don't care. Part of me says, "You can do it!" Part of me says it doesn't matter. I've never been so down, lost, frightened and confused.

We had yet to fully embrace the diagnosis, but I had become clinically depressed—and the triggers in my case had been the chronic pain, and the sleep deprivation that went along with it, and perhaps even the emotional stresses of the previous fall. Jonathan's illness. The pressures of work, and growing the Emme brand. Toby's birth. September 11. It was all rolled up and bundled together, and I was left feeling drained. I was so totally not myself, only this time the fatigue was even more pronounced than it had been over the winter. And it wasn't just fatigue. The mood swings were more apparent, the dark thoughts more troubling. And I was further "out of it" than ever before.

Let me slip in another few words on my family history with depression, because it's all-important. As I've mentioned, my brother Seth was in a pretty intense depression in his early twenties. In his case, it seemed to flow from a bad breakup with a girl he was supposed to marry. We were living with our parents at the time, in a "cool" bachelor pad we'd set up in their basement, and I remember having the hardest time dealing with how things were for my brother. I couldn't imagine how it was for him—that is, until I went through some of the same motions myself. But back then I was desperate to know what he was going through. We'd been pretty much joined at the hip since birth—and even longer than that, if you believe some of the research on the closeness of identical twins. When it came time for college, we went away to different schools—he went to Tulane, I went to Syracuse—but we actually worked together for a good chunk of that first year following graduation, playing guitar and singing as a duo called Mirror Images at small restaurants and clubs in Greenwich Village like Folk City, Speak Easy and the Bitter End, and touring the British and French West Indies for Club Med. The bad breakup came when we were about twenty-three years old, and it hit Seth superhard. It was Jonathan's senior year in high school, back before the first traces of the brain cancer that would mark the rest of our lives, and I remember thinking what a shame it was that Jonathan's senior year passed virtually unnoticed. Our attentions, as a family, were elsewhere. What should have been a joyous, celebratory time in Jonathan's life was set aside by Seth's suffering. We were all caught up in it. I can even remember these long discussions, during which my parents voiced their concerns that Seth's future might be stamped in some way by his depression. They ended up paying for his treatment out of pocket, because they didn't want there to be any record of it with our medical insurance company. They didn't want it to come up in a future job interview, or on any kind of background check. It wasn't something we talked about, outside of our few close friends, not because we were ashamed of it but because society put such a taboo on it. There was a stigma to it, back in the early 1980s, and things have gotten better in the past couple decades, but we're still not where we need to be on this one. That's the killing silence of mental illness—we're afraid to talk about it!—and I knew it firsthand, and we jumped through all kinds of hoops to ensure it would never come up for Seth in any context. There was a clear feeling he would get past it, but at the same time there was a fear that he might be held back because of it.

Whether we talked about it or not, Seth's suffering was my suffering, and yet at one point I felt I needed to get out of the house. It was too much for me to have to deal with, I thought at the time. I was still just a kid. I didn't have the strength. It killed me to see him so distraught. He used to beat the stuffing out of himself, in much the same way that I would do years later, and it tore me up inside to see him in such an agitated state. There was nothing I could do to help him, and yet after consulting with his doctor I came to realize that my leaving would very likely make Seth's prospects appear worse, so I stayed on and dug in. When things were bleakest, I used to hug him and tell him that he was going to get better, never once thinking that twenty years later he'd be hugging me and saying essentially the same thing.

During the few times we did get to talking about it as a family, we learned that my father's mother had been in and

out of depressions for much of her adult life. That was
Grandma Anna. My grandparents were good, hardworking
people; my grandfather was a kosher butcher, with a meat
shop on Featherbed Lane in the Bronx. My grandmother was
sweet, and loving, but there was frequently something *off*
about her. Everyone dismissed her behavior as "quirky." She
used to steal the plastic flowers from the lobbies of the great
apartment buildings on Ocean Parkway in Brooklyn and
rearrange them in her home. Also, she was a little obsessive
about cleanliness. That was her thing. If my father or his
brother dropped an item of clothing on the floor, it would go
straight into the wash—before it even had a chance to hit the
ground, it seemed to her kids. She was even known to wash
money and hang it on a clothesline to dry. (How's that for
giving "money laundering" a new twist?) At some point or
other, she underwent shock therapy, which at the time was
only given to patients suffering from severe forms of mental
illness. It was considered an extreme, last-resort type of treatment, and I remember she came home from the hospital and
stayed for a while at our house in Tenafly, and when she was
there she was endlessly out of it and hopelessly confused.
She didn't stay with us long, however. Soon, she moved into
a nursing home, but had to be transferred to another hospital
because she caused so much trouble with the other residents.
(Among other things, she told all of the residents that the
food was poisoned—and they believed her!)

Grandma Anna also had a sister—my great-aunt Bella—
who had to be institutionalized. She used to run around the
streets naked before her family had her committed, and she
lived out her days in the psych unit.

Indeed, depression ran all the way back to my great-grandmother Fanny, Grandma Anna's mother. I was named for her. In fact, if I had been a girl, that would have been my name . . . Fanny. Thank God I was a boy. Can you imagine having to grow up with the name Fanny? My mother used to say it wasn't Fanny with a short *a*; it was Fanny with an open *a*, as in "Fa la la la la." "Fanny, my ass!" I used to say. "I don't care how you pronounce it. It's still Ass!"

My great-grandmother Fanny was institutionalized at the Pilgrim State Hospital on Long Island, where she received some of the earliest shock therapy treatments in the New York area, back when it was considered a controversial and aggressive form of treatment.

In addition to her sister Bella, Grandma Anna had a number of sisters who suffered from depression, although in those days they didn't always diagnose depression by name. In those days, they were all just quirky, and the quirkiness ran to a couple of my father's cousins as well. There was even a suicide in my family tree: my great-grandfather Harry, a butcher and cattle farmer who got mixed up in a cattle-stealing scheme in the hills of South Jersey, had slit his own throat rather than face the charges against him.

This runaway family history of depression even ran to my dad, although he was able to function at a fairly high level through his depression, which in his case was brought about by a professional setback, and then exacerbated by Jonathan's first grand mal seizure, which revealed the mass on his brain. Imagine having to withstand something like that—losing your job, and watching your sons take turns falling to illness—if you're prone to depression in the first place, but to my father's great credit he came through it okay.

And yet even with all this common ground, my father's family never talked about their various struggles with depression. It wasn't until Seth's depression in the early 1980s that all these aunts and cousins began to come out of the woodwork and really reach out to my parents, and this was a great, good thing, because it helped us to put everything into perspective, and left us all better equipped to deal with it and to help Seth through the balance of his recovery because of what we'd learned about the Aronson genetic makeup.

It was no help to me, though, not when I was in the grip of it.

Oct. 21, '02

The day is what I'm making it. I feel drugged and out of control. What do I do? Where do I go? How do I act? I'm really losing it. I don't know what to do. Everyone is so supportive, yet I can't support myself. I'm taking new meds. Maybe they'll help. I need to help myself but I can't. I want to, but I can't. I don't have the strength . . . Doctor's visit this morning was one big fog. How did I get into the city? Drove, I guess. Can't remember . . . I'm so confused. I'm tired. I want to go to sleep and wake up better. It's not going to happen. How long do I need to go? Can't seem to turn it around.

Speaking Up

L ooking back, it's hard to understand how we made so many mistakes with Phil's chronic pain, how our focus had been so off. Each step of the way, we thought we were making the right next move, but we were so long without answers, so long without any clear course of action that there was never any clear-cut consensus on what the right next move ought to be.

It sometimes seemed like all we had managed to collect from Phil's many consultations and examinations was a string of ambiguous comments. There was no clear-cut diagnosis or treatment plan. No one could pinpoint what was happening to Phil, or why, or what we might do to see him safely to the other side of it . . . whatever *it* was.

It's a wearying, heartbreaking thing, to see the person you love, your partner, in such constant agony, and to know that there's nothing you can do for him that carried any certainty of actually working. Dr. Wharton did a tremendous job for Phil, but there were times early on when I wanted to scream at him to do more. He helped us put together a great team of doctors, and he was very much a team player, but I sometimes wanted him to be a little less conservative in prescribing medications, and a little more proactive in Phil's treatment.

Here's one thing I learned from our giant mess: in areas of mental health, it's very important to make a strong personal connection with your doctors. It's not like going to see an internist, or an orthopedist. It's an intimate relationship. Referrals are great, but you need to shop around to make sure the person you're working with is a good fit. Your personalities have to mesh, and your approaches to treatment should be in sync as well. Phil made a great connection with Dr. Wharton, even as I worried we should be a little more aggressive in his treatment, so we looked to build on that connection to help Phil get better. If you have the luxury, take the time to interview a bunch of doctors before settling on any one of them. Once you connect, and once you're convinced you've made the right choice, be respectful of your doctor's time. Be prepared with questions going into each visit. Write everything down—not just what you think you understand, but what you don't understand as well. Don't worry about looking stupid or not knowing what the heck is going on. Just keep asking those questions, and keep writing!

I used to get these killer hand cramps after our sessions with Dr. Wharton, because I was scribbling so furiously in this little notebook I carried with me to all of our appointments. Dosages, treatments plans, referrals to other specialists . . . I wrote it all down. I took being Phil's advocate very seriously, although in retrospect I could have been a better advocate for Phil's pain management. I could have taken the lead on this one. After all, Phil was in no shape to speak up for himself, or to think things through in any kind of clear way, and I should have spoken up on his behalf. I should have seen things more clearly.

It's the one aspect that keeps me up nights, all this time later, because a part of me believes that if we'd found a way to get the pain under control, the depression might not have hit Phil so hard or so suddenly. I've got no real idea whether this is actually the case, but that's what I came away thinking. It's one of the classic side effects when a couple goes through a major illness like a depression. Usually, there's something the healthy partner finds to feel guilty about, and I guess this is my guilt trip. There's also a school of thought that suggests marriage to someone in a depression is a kind of codependency, but I don't know what to make of this one. Yes, I knew some of Phil's family history of depression before we decided to make a life together, but I couldn't know that it would hit him—us!—so hard. He was so fine, so on top of everything, for so many years, I had no real reason to think he'd follow this same path, so I have to cut myself some slack. Was I blinded by love in such a way that it kept me from seeing Phil's picture clearly? I don't think so. I know the literature suggests that the depression would have found Phil eventually, and I know that if it wasn't the chronic pain that brought it on it would have been something else, some other trigger, probably sometime soon. Phil's doctors all said the same thing. But did either of us see this coming? No way.

In any case, I know I did the best I could for Phil, and he knows it too, even though if we had it to do differently we'd move more aggressively on the pain management front, most definitely.

Initially, our thinking was that if Phil were to get pain management early on for the chronic pain, he would either become addicted to the painkillers or he would mask the symptoms to such a degree that it would be virtually impossible to diagnose the underlying problem. Who knew? Now, looking back, I can say with conviction that you need to cut the pain so you can deal with life. It's Job One, really. If you're lucky, you'll find doctors who will be your advocates in this area as well—doctors who practice humanism in medicine. (To learn more about this all-important area, consult www.humanism-in-medicine.org, a valuable Web site for patients and families in all areas of the country looking for compassionate care.)

Since the goal of this book is to help others suffering through their own ordeals, I want to emphasize the point. If something feels *not right*, take care of it straightaway, and if a clear-cut diagnosis is not quick in coming, step things up until one is. If something is so completely off the map of your experience that you don't recognize it, get a new map. Don't rely exclusively on word-of-mouth recommendations or suggestions or homeopathic remedies from friends and family, and don't wait around for a doctor with all the answers to magically appear. There are no magic answers or cure-all treatments, so read everything you can. Talk to everyone you can. Become as much of an expert as you possibly can, as quickly as you can, and take total charge. For most of us, the best sounding board or clearinghouse for advice and counsel will be our family doctor, and that's a great place to start, but this is a time to tap your network of friends and family and professional contacts. This is a time to call in the heavy artillery.

Connect every dot.

Consider every possibility.

Cover every base.

Yes, we missed the boat when it came to diagnosing and treating Phil's penile pain, and we nearly missed the boat when it came time to seek psychiatric help, too, because I don't know that we would have connected with Dr. Wharton if we didn't already have an ongoing relationship with him through Phil's family. Phil put off the idea of a psychiatric consultation for the longest time, and when I finally pressed him on it he continued to resist. He thought he had everything under control, and that it was all tied in to the pain. That was the way he got through it, I guess, believing that if he could just find a way to cope with the constant burning sensation, he'd be okay. Ultimately, we didn't reach out to Dr. Wharton so much as he reached out to us. See, Dr. Wharton had helped Phil's brother Seth get through his depression in 1986, and continued to treat Seth over the years, and he had lately been working with the family to help everyone prepare for the pain of losing Jonathan. Actually, it was at the end of one of these family sessions that Seth stepped in and asked if we could spend some time on what was going on with Phil. It was almost like an intervention.

Seth had been down this road before, and he saw where Phil was headed, and he gave us the gentle push we desperately needed.

Here again, I don't know what we were waiting for. It was August or so before we made our own appointment to see Dr. Wharton, away from the rest of the family. That was about four months into this relentless nightmare of pain, and long past the time when Phil first started showing signs of depression. All along, we'd been thinking we were taking a proactive approach to Phil's treatment, but if we had been *really* on top of things, if we had *really* covered every angle, we might have sought out someone like Dr. Wharton the previous fall, when Phil was first going through that weird, Epstein-Barr-like fatigue, to see if there was any psychological component to that. At the very least, we should have consulted someone once it was clear that the constant penile pain was taking an emotional toll, and started in with some antidepressants and some therapy—probably back in June or July, when the pain was long past the point of intolerable—but that wasn't the direction we were going in. We were a little naive, I guess, and a little too trusting, and I suppose we figured that if we determined the cause of the pain everything else would take care of itself.

Let me tell you, that *so* wasn't the way to go, but that's the way we went, and by the time Dr. Wharton began treating Phil for depression he was pretty far gone. The bizarre thing with how it happened for Phil was that he seemed to swap one bad patch for another—all of a sudden. It's like the chronic pain and the depression traded places. One week, he was overwhelmed by the pain, and barely functioning, and the next week he was just overwhelmed, and barely functioning for a whole different set of reasons. In fact, the first idea I had of how deeply and swiftly he'd fallen into depression was a tossed-off comment he made one night. He said, "Emme, as bad as that was, with the burning and everything else, I'd take it in a second over what I'm feeling right now."

I heard that and thought, *Whoa, what are we into here?* You have to realize, up until that moment, I'd known Phil was down, and not himself. Even with the rose-colored blinders we seemed to have put on with this thing, I could see he'd need some time, and the right combination of medications, to set things right. I knew things were about to get tough, like they had with his brother Seth. I was not yet in the picture when Seth was in his depression, but I'd heard all the stories and started to get some idea what we might be facing. We were already seeing Dr. Wharton by this point, and talking about Phil's condition as a depression, and experimenting with our first cocktail of antidepressants. But I'd also known how much Phil had struggled the previous six months or so. I'd seen him climbing the walls, ready to tear his hair out over that constant pain. I'd *felt* it, if such a thing was possible, and to hear him say that he would choose that obvious agony over the less-obvious turmoil he was going through at just that moment . . . well, it broke my heart all over again, and just about scared the crap right out of me, because I knew right then we were in for a serious battle.

When the chronic pain was at its very worst, Phil used to rattle on dejectedly about finding his way out of the pain.

He'd say things like "Oh, Emme, I just want to die," which—incredibly!—I didn't hear as a suicidal thought. Not at first, anyway. To me, it sounded like somebody saying, "Oh, I've had it with this pain." You know, like a plaintive cry. We've all said things like that from time to time, or we've all heard someone say something similar without becoming too alarmed. It's like a throwing up of hands, a plea for help. In Phil's case, though, his despairing cries got more and more specific. They went from "I just want to die" to "I could just crawl under that rock" to "I think I could wrap my car around that tree." It started to freak me out, but by the time we'd get around to really talking about it, the impulse behind his disturbingly specific comment would have passed and Phil would say he was just venting. Over time, though, this was one area where Phil's signs of distress eventually became transparent. When things were at their very bleakest, in the spring and summer of 2003, he was tossing off these suicidal comments every hour or so, and by this time there was no mistaking them for anything else. They peppered his every conversation. He was constantly wondering what combination of pills he'd need to take, or figuring how fast he'd need to be driving heading into a collision, or talking about what would happen if he jumped off the George Washington Bridge . . . gruesome, graphic stuff like that. He'd share these thoughts like they were nothing at all, and when I would then share them with Dr. Wharton or friends and family, I'd be told not to worry, or that it was just the depression talking. Of course, I realize that everyone was just trying to be helpful, and everyone had our best interests at heart, but how could I *not* worry?

This was my husband, actively and openly fantasizing about killing himself. Of course, it was just the depression talking—*that's* why I was absolutely sick with worry.

As we turned the corner into 2003, there wasn't even time to breathe any kind of sigh now that the penile pain had finally gone. I ached for Phil, and everything he endured, and the carrot at the end of the stick had been the relief I knew he would feel when the inflammation in his prostate area finally subsided. We longed for that relief, but by the time it finally came we were on to the next worry, which was seeing our way through Phil's depression. There was no letup.

Whenever we consulted a new doctor, I brought my little notepad with me and wrote down everything we talked about. Diagnoses. Suggested courses of action. New meds we might consider if this next course didn't do the trick. It was something I learned from my mother-in-law, Judy, from all those years taking care of Jonathan, running in and out of all these doctors' offices. I felt I needed to stay on top of things, to really understand our treatment plan, what the medications were meant to do, things like that.

I also began to track our considerable expenses. Fortunately, our insurance covered most of it, but the out-of-pocket costs associated with Phil's care soon grew to be enormous, topping out at over $75,000 by the time we were through, to cover copayments and certain medications and doctor and hospital visits outside our plan. One of our biggest decisions, relative to insurance, was whether to continue seeing Dr. Wharton on such a long-term, open-ended basis, because he was not in our insurance plan, but Phil and I both came to feel that we couldn't see our way to the other side of this ordeal without him. And if that weren't enough, the *total* cost of Phil's care, as of this writing, was approaching $500,000, a staggering number that will continue to grow as Phil continues with his antidepressants and his ongoing psychiatric consultations. We took the attitude that the money wasn't anything but a means to an end, and that nothing was more important than Phil's recovery, but I kept thinking about all those people who don't have health insurance, or those who couldn't afford to make the kind of out-of-network, out-of-pocket decisions we were able to make. What would we have done, I wondered, if we couldn't have chosen the doctors or the treatment plan we felt were right for Phil? How would we have managed? The associated costs of mental health care—indeed, of health care in general—is a giant issue in our society, and we never lost sight of how lucky we were in this regard. We'd been fairly successful in our careers. We had a nice house, in a nice neighborhood, but we still needed to work to stay ahead of our bills, and soon enough it got to where the medical bills left us pretty tapped out. Phil didn't pay much attention to the money at the time, as you might imagine, but he wasn't so far gone that he couldn't recognize the terrible inequity in the system. He came home from the drugstore one day completely rattled by the cost of his medications. The pharmacist had presented him with a bill for $325 for his latest meds, which I guess would have covered fourteen to twenty-one days of treatment, neglecting to credit the charge to our insurance. And that was just for his psych meds; he'd picked up his heart and pain medications on a separate visit. Once Phil pointed out the mistake, the copayment charge came to *only* $35, but even that can add up to a lot of money on a year-round basis.

Hand in hand with the notes and the expense ledger, I started writing down some observations at home, whenever there was something worth noting. It wasn't a journal in any kind of traditional sense, but I wanted to remind myself what we were doing, or thinking, at a particular time. I wanted to chart Phil's progress—or, what I *hoped* would be Phil's progress, because he certainly wasn't making any just yet. Looking back over those observations now, all this time later, I'm reminded how determined we were to keep up appearances—anyway, to continue with our usual routines. For example, in November 2002, when Phil's depression now sat alongside the chronic pain as a front-and-center worry, I dragged Phil to the opening of the Eric Carle Museum of Picture Book Art, in Amherst, Massachusetts. I say *dragged* because Phil didn't need to be there as much as I needed him to be there, if that makes any sense. Eric Carle, the noted illustrator and author of such classic children's books as *The Very Hungry Caterpillar* and *The Very Grouchy Ladybug*, was a dear friend. He was involved with my mother for about three years, when I was a little girl, and he had been a big part of my life; we'd reconnected just after the publication of my first book, *True Beauty*, and he and his wife, Bobbie, had been wonderful to us ever since. I felt I had to be there—and at the same time I thought it would be good for Phil to get out of the house and make the effort to socialize. Even through the fog of depression, Phil knew how important it was to me to be on hand for the museum opening, and he knew I couldn't leave him alone, so he found the strength to make the trip, which I took as an encouraging sign.

At least, I was encouraged until we got to Amherst, where Phil suddenly became all anxious and sweaty and jittery. When we got to the hotel, he changed his clothes a few times, for no real reason, and then at some point he threw up his hands and decided he couldn't leave the room. It took our good friend Mark, who was accompanying us on this trip, to literally drag Phil out of bed and into a set of appropriate clothes, and amazingly Phil didn't put up any kind of struggle. He was like a rag doll as Mark helped to get him dressed.

Naturally, I would become all too familiar with this type of unpredictable nervous behavior, but it was still relatively new to us in November 2002, so I didn't know what to make of it. I tried to calm Phil down, in whatever ways I could think. He was now dressed, but I still couldn't get him out the door of our hotel room. I tried to explain where we were, and what we were meant to be doing, and I reminded him how important it was for us to be present for Eric and Bobbie. I tried to demonstrate to Phil that he was being irrational, and that the depression was clouding his perspective.

At dinner, Phil was seated next to a guest who kept calling him on his admittedly strange behavior, and I looked on and fought back tears over the way my sick husband must have seemed to all these people. He'd always been such an engaging, gregarious person in these types of social settings—great-looking, and charming, and all those good things—and here he was, sweating profusely, unable to focus, wanting to be anywhere else but at this table. He made an effort to contribute to the conversation, but his attempts fell mostly flat, like there was a connection missing between the moment he thought of something to say and the moment he got around to saying it.

That was to be one of our last "social" outings for the next year or so, and once we got back to New Jersey there was nothing to do but watch helplessly as Phil slipped deeper and deeper into this strange new mode. Once again, as he'd done the previous fall, he started staying in bed later and later each morning, only by this time it was virtually impossible to get him up and out and dressed. His moods were up and down and everywhere in between. His appetite became hit or miss. There were times when he would eat way too much food, and other times when he wouldn't eat at all. For a couple weeks, he went through this really weird anorexic stage. The more he seemed to lose control of every other aspect of his life, the more he seemed to want to control this one. He started playing with his food—not *playing* with it the way a child might at the dinner table, but messing around with its importance to his overall health, and changing his eating habits in ways that had nothing to do with his body or his appetite. Typically, a textbook anorexic will look in the mirror and get back an image that doesn't quite correspond to what another person might see. Their body image is all askew. And here Phil was losing all this weight and thinking he had gotten terribly fat. He'd dropped about thirty or forty pounds, and he was skinny as a rail, and he still sat in front of the mirror for hours, bitching about his appearance, pinching his belly and feeling certain he was too flabby around the middle.

He had no energy, no appetite, no drive . . . and all of this was in such sharp contrast to how he usually was. He was depriving himself of everything, and when you don't nourish yourself—physically, intellectually, or emotionally—your body tends to shut down. That's what was happening with Phil. He couldn't sleep at night. He couldn't engage with the rest of the world. He couldn't even connect with me or Toby. If I ask him about it now, he has no real recollection of what was going through his head during this time, but he seemed so out of it, like he was someplace else.

One of the things Dr. Wharton suggested to ease Phil past this down period was to give him certain chores to do around the house, little doses of responsibility I thought he could handle. In this way, we hoped, Phil would find some extra motivation to get out of bed each morning, and to put one foot in front of the other and make some forward progress each day. They'd be something to do, these tasks, and after they were accomplished they would also be a boost to his self-esteem, which was really flagging. The most doable job I could think of was to have Phil make the bed each morning, which was certainly something he could handle, and which served the double purpose of forcing him out of it in order to make it.

At some point early on Phil told me he thought he could handle taking Toby to a little music class she took in town.

I thought, *Okay, great, now we're getting somewhere.* So that's what he did, for a time, until he came home one afternoon and confided that he had no real idea how he'd gotten back and forth to and from the class. It's like he was sleepwalking his way through life—only he was doing it behind the wheel of a car, with our little daughter on board! I panicked, and I'm afraid that in my panic I dragged Phil into panic mode right along with me.

(Obviously, that was the last time he drove—with Toby, or anyone else for that matter—but by this point he'd already put himself and every other driver on the road in harm's way so many times it's a wonder they're all still alive, as Phil will soon make clear.)

Another time, I left him on the outside porch watching Toby, while I stepped inside to take a shower, thinking he had the situation covered. He'd always been an attentive father, even during the worst of his pain, so I went inside without a thought, and when I stepped out of the shower, just a few minutes later, I heard a scream. I rushed downstairs to find Toby crying and bleeding from a cut on her chin, and Phil was standing in the corner with his head down. Toby was fine, just cut up a little bit, but the really troubling part was Phil's reaction: there wasn't any. He was more bewildered than concerned. He hadn't rushed to her side, or called for me to come down to help. He just stayed off to himself, looking on silently at the scene, looking a little confused and like he'd let us all down. What happened was Toby was climbing on a wrought iron chaise we had out on the porch, and Phil knew she wasn't supposed to be climbing on it, but he must have been powerless to pull her down from her perch. He saw her, and he knew what he had to do, but he simply couldn't bring himself to do it— and so, inevitably, she fell. I was furious, but at the same time I was mad at myself for being furious. It wasn't Phil's fault for allowing Toby to climb on the chaise; it was mine for leaving Toby alone with him.

It was a clarifying moment, and I realized he could no longer watch Toby. Everything changed with that incident. The logistics of running our household. My ability to work. Everything. Somebody needed to be with Phil at all times, and that somebody needed to be me. I tried to talk to him about it. I said, "Honey, if the house was burning, and you were alone with Toby, and she was upstairs, would you be able to go up and get her?"

He said, "Em, I'm not sure I could even get myself out."

And right then I knew we were into this thing pretty deep. Right then I knew nothing would be the same.

The medications were a constant concern, and here's where all that note-taking came in. Phil's doctors were trying to get a fix on his situation, and each week they would tweak his medications ever so slightly, and monitor him to see how he reacted. They'd alter the dosage by the tiniest amount, or they'd switch him to a new medication entirely, or decide they didn't like how one drug was interacting with the meds he had to take for his atrial fibrillation, or his cholesterol. It was a constant puzzle, and it was all tied together. Phil didn't exactly help himself in this one area, because he started playing around with his own dosages, according to his mood or his inexplicable whims. Some nights, he wouldn't take the Ambien meant to help him sleep, because he felt like he didn't need it—which of course meant that he wouldn't sleep that night. Other nights, if he was worried sleep wouldn't come, he'd double up on his dosage. It was such a mess, but Dr. Wharton was big into letting Phil be in charge of taking his own medications. I understood the impulse to give Phil some autonomy in this area, but the reality was that he just wasn't up to it, and I started to feel strongly that I should be the one dispensing Phil's medications. But Dr. Wharton would keep saying, "Emme, you've got to let Phil take some responsibility on this one. We can't take everything away from him. He needs to do this for himself."

So that's what we did, for a time.

Each day, it seemed, we'd lose another piece of Phil. It happened in such small increments, it was barely noticeable from one day to the next. It was only over a stretch of days or weeks that I could look back and see how much he'd changed, how far he'd fallen, how desperate our situation had become. I began to think we'd have to hit bottom before we could climb our way back up and out, before someone would hit the "reset" button and give us a second chance to start anew. But then I'd look up a week or so later and realize we'd fallen further still. There was no end to it, and I remember thinking that no one else could see what I could see. No one knew what it was like, to be caught up in it like we were. We had an amazing group of supportive friends, and our families couldn't have been more caring, but it's a lonely thing to be married to a man in the depths of a depression with an infant daughter at home. I'd always been a social animal, and I made my living in a very people-oriented way, but here I had to shut down my usual routines and alter my outlook on life and the world around me. It was all about *us* and *them*. It was all about getting through each day.

I'd never felt more alone.

Exit Strategies

PHIL

Okay, so I was a reluctant customer when it came time to see a psychiatrist. Dr. Wharton was a great guy, and from everything I could tell he was an amazing therapist. Our family had known him for years and years, but it took me a while to recognize that he could help me. It took Emme's gentle persistence, and it took Seth telling Dr. Wharton about my chronic pain, and my trouble dealing, and how I was spiraling downhill and out of control. I don't know that I would have chosen just those words to describe myself and what I was going through at that time, but I have to admit they were pretty accurate. Seth had been there before. He knew what he was talking about.

The first thing Dr. Wharton did once I was in his care was prescribe the antidepressant Elavil, which was meant to increase the level of serotonin in my brain. It was also supposed to have some analgesic properties, to help with some of the still-chronic pain, but I don't think it did anything for me from a pain standpoint. Anyway, I didn't notice any significant change, although Emme and I were probably a little too impatient for our own good. We were so deep into it that we longed for immediate results, but that's not how it works. I knew as much, and so did Emme, but that didn't seem to matter to us just then. You have to give these medications time, especially since I was already taking all those meds for my heart condition, and Dr. Wharton could not have been clearer about this, but in my head I didn't have a whole lot of time. In my head, I needed to get better immediately, because I couldn't go on like this.

Immediately was a long way off, and in the meantime I tried to establish and stick to some routines. First and foremost, of course, was staying on top of my medications. That got to be pretty much a full-time job, and I didn't know if I was up to it at first. I was on so many different drugs that I needed a pillbox and a list of instructions to keep them straight. Morning, noon, and night, I'd set out my pills and swallow them down, and then I'd wait to see if anything happened. It's like I was in a movie, and I expected special effects. I *longed* for special effects—anything that would take me from the grip of misery I was in. Each time, it was a huge disappointment when I didn't notice any changes, even though I knew that any positive change would be gradual, and cumulative, and probably unnoticeable even to me. It could take weeks, or months, before we'd see any improvement, maybe even longer—but still, I was disappointed, so much so that the days began to run into each other. There was no way to mark the time, except for the taking of my pills. Morning, noon, and night. On and on and on. When one vial emptied, there'd be another prescription to take its place. It's like there was a bottomless well of pills, and the meds were my calendar, my clock on the wall, my one important thing to do each day.

I stayed in bed a lot, although I don't think I slept all that much. Oh, I slept, but it wasn't the kind of deep, restful sleep I so desperately craved; rather, I nodded in and out, dimly aware of whatever else was going on in my room, or just outside my window. I was constantly and endlessly and restlessly tired. I could have stayed in bed forever—and I damn near did just that. Sleep was my only shot at any kind of relief, even fitful sleep, because it took me away from the anguish and uncertainty. I tried to exercise, when I felt up to it, because Dr. Wharton insisted I make the effort. I ran. I rode my bike. I went to the gym. Seth got me started with a trainer, and tried to drag me to the gym at least a couple times a week. I went through all the right motions, whenever I could, even though my head was someplace else. Some weeks, I couldn't exercise at all. Some weeks, I'd manage to do something each day. It was a scattershot kind of deal, and most all the time the *idea* of exercising weighed so heavily on me that I did nothing at all.

Toby was my motivation. I forced myself to be at least some kind of father to her. Not every day, mind you, and not in the ways I had once imagined, but I was in no position to quibble. I took whatever my illness gave me. I brought her with me on some of my runs in her little jogging stroller—when the weather was nice enough, when I felt up to the responsibility. She snuggled with me in bed, when I couldn't get my head off the pillow. I tried to make my way into the kitchen at least once a day, timed to whenever Emme was feeding her. Some days, I even managed to feed her myself. I tried to make it to the bathroom when she was being bathed. But there was so much I missed, and it began to gnaw at me—not in a front-and-center kind of way, but deep down, in the places where you think about things you don't like to think about. I missed Toby's first little steps, and her first words, and a whole bunch of other milestones—because most days I couldn't even get out of bed. There was all of this exciting, once-in-a-lifetime stuff happening with Toby, and I was close enough to taste it— hell, I was living in the same house!—but at the same time so far out of it that it barely registered.

Every morning, Emme would bring Toby into our bedroom and try to get me out of bed. If I cared to notice, they looked like something out of a Normal Rockwell painting, all innocence and sunshine and hope. By contrast, I must have looked like something out of a Stephen King novel. I wished like hell I could pay attention. I wished I could peel back the pain and jump out of the picture I'd made for myself and into the one with Emme and Toby.

They'd throw open the shades and sing this cute little song:

Good morning to you,
Good morning to you,
We're all in our places.
With bright shiny faces . . .

I'd hear them, underneath whatever silent fog I'd slipped into during the night, and I'd catch a glimpse from out of the corner of the eye I was pretending to keep closed, and I'd want desperately to reach out to them, to take my place alongside them, but I couldn't move a muscle. The effort was too great, too daunting. Can you imagine what that's like? To have your beautiful wife and daughter come into your room each morning to sing you awake, to want to reach out to them and collect them in a hug and get started on a wonderful new day together, and to not have the strength or the wherewithal to pull it off? It was like being buried alive. I knew that all I had to do was lift my head off the pillow, or open just one eyelid, or whisper some sort of greeting, and my two girls would be on me in a flash, filling me in on their day's plans, but I couldn't even manage that.

One eyelid! A whisper! That's how incapacitating it can be, to be in a depression, to be focused enough to know what you're missing and yet too far gone to do anything about it.

Most days, it took four or five trips into our room for Emme to get me up and out and moving around. Some days, it took more than that. She'd try everything. In the beginning, she used to bring Toby in with her each and every time, and they'd sing their little song, but after a while I guess that got kind of old. "Okay, Em," I'd say. "I get it. I'm up. Just give me a sec." And then she'd disappear and I'd close my eyes and forget she'd just been there, hoping to steal another couple hours of sleep until Emme returned to check up on me. I craved the quiet and stillness of my bedroom, even if I couldn't fall asleep, and I tried every trick in the book to stay there as much as possible. This went on all morning, sometimes into the afternoon. And there were many days when I didn't bother to get out of bed at all.

I was supposed to make the bed each day, but a lot of times I'd do a half-assed job of it and then slip right back under the sheets. Other days, I'd feign illness—a stomachache, or a virus, or a cold—and tell Emme I needed to stay in bed. She bought these appeals, for a time, but after a while they got kind of old, too. After a while, she was on to me; plus, her patience and good cheer began to grow thin, which I guess was understandable, with what I was putting her through. It got to where she'd end up storming into the room, screaming, "Phil, get out of bed!" Like she didn't have time for any more of my crap. And then she'd hurl the covers onto the floor and say, "You need to get up! Now!" And so I'd have no choice but to get out of bed and make like I was getting dressed, or putting on my sneakers to go for a run, but as soon as Emme left the room to look after Toby I'd shut down again. And the thing of it is, all during this time, my mind never once stopped racing. I couldn't get the rest of my body to do a damn thing, but my thoughts were all over the place. I kept thinking about how horrible I felt, how I hated my life, how I hated me, how easy it would be to put an end to all my suffering. I loved the life Emme and I had built together, but I hated what it had become, what *I* had become.

A friend of mine came by during this period and told me a joke. The punch line was "When you get up in the morning, if you can't put your feet on the ground, half your problems are over, and if you can't put your feet on the ground, all your problems are over." It didn't strike me as all that funny, but it was certainly meaningful, and every morning after I heard it the line kept racing through my head as I tried to get out of bed. *Come on, Phil,* I'd tell myself. *Put your feet on the ground and your problems will really be over.* It seemed so simple, and yet at the same time it was impossible.

Other friends came by and took turns trying to cajole me out of bed and out into the world. Seth would come over and try to drag me to some activity, or distract me with some new song he'd just heard, or some piece of family news or gossip. There was always something he wanted to share. Sometimes, he'd climb onto the bed alongside me, and we'd lay there in silence, the way we used to do as kids, when his bed was closer to the air-conditioning and we'd take shifts in front of the vents to share the cool air. Or my mother would come by with Jonathan, and he'd do what he could to lift my spirits. The very fact that my sick little brother wanted to be there, that he would make the supreme effort to be supportive at a time when he could barely move or talk or take care of himself, was almost embarrassing—for the in-your-face reminder that *he* felt he needed to take care of *me*—but that's where we were with this thing. I should have been heading over to my parents' house, to give Jonathan a lift, but here he was reaching out to me.

My good friend Dan came over one afternoon and tried to get me to sit through the latest *Lord of the Rings* movie. I didn't want to go to a movie, but he said, "I don't care. You're coming." There was a time when I would have liked nothing more than to kill an afternoon watching an epic, fantasy-type movie, so I went. I ended up leaving about ten minutes into it, because all those sights and sounds were just too overwhelming. Plus, Dan told me later that I seemed scared by that Golum creature on the screen, almost like a child would be frightened by the eerie, creepy voice. I can still remember that feeling of sheer anxiety, although the specifics are lost to the depression; in any case, I needed to leave, because Dan said I seemed freaked. But it was important that I went. It was important that I was surrounded by friends and family who cared enough to push me out the door. Remember Hillary Clinton's book, in which she talked about how it takes a village to raise a child? Well, it takes a village—and then some!—to help someone through a depression, and I was blessed to live among such loving, caring, supportive villagers. Sure, some of the *natives* got a little restless, and threw up their hands at what must have seemed to all concerned like frustrating behavior, but they were there for me the entire way, and I wouldn't be here to write this account were it not for their amazing extra efforts.

I tried to put what I was experiencing into some kind of context, to gain some perspective on it. When I was able to think clearly, I thought about my depression in terms of work. I'd had a whole bunch of jobs in my professional career—advertising, sales, graphic design, management— and I was never intimidated by any of them because I always told myself that all businesses are the same, and all people are the same. It doesn't matter what industry you're working in, or who your colleagues or bosses are, as long as you know your stuff, and I always followed my four simple rules: one, *believe in yourself*; two, *if you don't ask, you don't get*; three, *if you know where you're going, you will most likely get there*; and four, *if you don't know how to get there, find someone who does*. And so, even when I was out of my element or in over my head, I was able to surround myself with people who could help me adjust—only here, with my depression, I was so far out of my element and so completely *out* of my head that I didn't know where to turn. I couldn't believe in myself; I didn't know what questions to ask or what answers I was seeking; I knew where I wanted to go, but I didn't have the first idea how to get there; and I couldn't find anyone to show me the way. Seth had been there—the person I'd been closest to my entire life! my other half!—but I wouldn't let him light a path for me because I refused to believe that what he experienced was what I was experiencing.

I was completely lost, and the best way I can think to describe how things were is to say there was too much weight bearing down on me. It's like I'd been sitting down, minding my own business, and someone handed me a five-hundred-pound barbell and said, "Okay, Phil, lift this up and move it over there." It was just not going to happen. It was physically impossible, beyond my capability, and that's the difficult aspect of depression, recognizing that your capabilities have undergone this dramatic shift, for no apparent reason, while at the same time recognizing that they will return to you once the illness has run its course. That's the killing part, because a great many people don't trust that the depression will lift. I know I didn't. I know I kept hearing Dr. Wharton, Emme, Seth, my mom and dad and everyone else telling me to ride it out and hang in there, that I was going to get better, but I never once thought I'd make it through. I thought I was doomed.

Here's another description, which came to me much, much later, after I'd attempted suicide and spent weeks and weeks on the psych ward and months and months in therapy and finally gotten back to being myself. I heard it on the radio, in that Green Day song "Give Me Novocaine," and it stuck: "It's like a throbbing toothache of the mind, I can't take this feeling anymore."

That about summed it up—and so did the following journal entry:

> Oct. 28, '02
> I'm feeling guilty because I don't feel like a man. I feel weak and vulnerable. I feel like I need someone to hold my hand. I want to get better but I'm fighting myself. I feel drugged and out of it . . .

I remember feeling so ashamed, like I was letting everybody down, and I look back now and think, *What the hell did I have to be ashamed about?* I mean, if I had cancer, I would not have been ashamed. If I had a heart attack, I would not have been ashamed. If I'd been hit by a bus, I would not have been ashamed. (Actually, maybe this last is a bad example, because I ached to be hit by a bus, but that's for a bit later on in this account.) That's the stigma I wrote about earlier, the mistaken notion that's still out there about depression, that it's something you can control, something to be ashamed about. Remember, I grew up in a family that reinforced this notion, paying for Seth's treatment out of pocket so there wouldn't be a record of it with his insurance company—not because there was anything for Seth to be ashamed about, but because the rest of the world might not have seen it the same way. Still, how ridiculous was that? To think there was something to hide? That the insurance police would come gunning for Seth and deny him his next job? And we Aronsons were presumably an educated, enlightened bunch, so you can just imagine how it sometimes goes in other, less open-minded households.

As far as controlling the depression—believe me, there's no controlling it. It controls you. And in my case it just reached up out of the depths of my chronic pain and took hold. There was nothing I could do about it.

The focus of each week were my appointments with Dr. Wharton. I saw him twice a week, through most of that fall. Emme would come with me, and she'd try to make an outing of it. She'd always suggest we stop for lunch, or run a couple errands, just to make sure I kept busy and distracted and circulating among active, healthy people. I always resisted. I looked forward to my sessions with Dr. Wharton, but at the same time I hated to see him. It reminded me that I wasn't well. Also, our time together was always so negative, and I realized at some point that I kept covering the same ground. Each visit was like an instant replay of the one before. I'd say the same things over and over again. *When am I going to get better? I want to kill myself. When am I going to get better? I want to kill myself . . .* I was like a broken record, like the boy who cried wolf. Yes, I was constantly talking about killing myself, but it's important to realize that these weren't empty threats. This was me, trying to build up the courage to actually pull it off. This was me, telling myself there was a way out of the pain and the depression and the suffocating confusion. This was me, taking charge and fighting back in the only way I knew how.

You'll see, tomorrow I'm not going to be here. You'll see . . .

Each week, my talk became more and more substantive, my impulses more and more real, but I'd laid such a foundation of nonsense that nobody took me seriously. Emme told me later that at some point she began to feel terrified that I was really going to take my own life—and I heard that from a place of health and emotional stability and thought, *Well, yeah . . . that was always the whole point.*

But I *was* a broken record. I *was* the boy who cried wolf. I don't know how Dr. Wharton put up with me—or with any of his other depressed patients, who were undoubtedly repeating their versions of the same thing. And Dr. Wharton was repeating himself too! I guess he was just hoping that his message—to put *something* into action—would finally hit home.

One of the great things about the healthy lifestyle Emme and I practiced was the way it drew us to so many like-minded people. Most of our friends are active, and physically fit, and a great many of them take a certain holistic approach to their well-being. The downside to this, though, was that everyone seemed to have a surefire cure-all to the chronic pain, when I was in the middle of it, and even to my depression, and I found myself feeling a little stressed out by all of their "helpful" suggestions. I called

Dr. Wharton every time someone contacted us with some new remedy, and he was patient with me at first, but after a while he thought all of this holistic-type experimenting was getting out of control. He said it was interfering with the carefully chosen cocktail of drugs he was prescribing. The juicing, the herbs, the vitamins . . . he wanted me to set that stuff aside and leave the treatment to him, and I was happy to let him guide me on this one. Emme and I came away thinking he was on top of things, as far as my meds were concerned. He might have been a little conservative with the dosages, particularly in the beginning, but we had no choice but to trust him completely.

Getting the right mix of medications into my system was a priority. I used to sit with Dr. Wharton in his office while he punched all this data into a computer-type machine he had to assess the various properties of my various medications, and to determine how they might interact with each other. There was some concern early on that my heart medications and my pain medications might not mix very well with the antidepressants he wanted to prescribe. Plus, there was some research to suggest that some of the beta-blockers I'd been taking the previous six years for my afib might contribute in some way to depression, so those meds were in play as well. In fact, working in conjunction with Dr. Wharton, my cardiologist, Dr. Lewis, took me off three of my heart medications (Toprol, Sectral, and Verapimil) and started experimenting with new ones.

Dr. Wharton told me at the outset that he wanted me to feel free to contact him outside our scheduled appointments, and these phone calls soon became a constant part of our doctor-patient relationship. Emme was always telling me how I needed to write down my questions, and not bother him about every little thing, but Dr. Wharton had a real open-door policy with his patients, and I took full advantage of it. When I was deeper into my depression, and feeling like I might harm myself, I would call him up and he would talk me down from my dark impulses. Sometimes I'd call him ten times a day, and looking back I can't imagine how he made all that time for me, and all his other patients besides, how he was able to keep track of each of our cases, down to the minutest detail. He was literally on call all the time.

People ask me all the time to describe a typical day when I was mired in my depression, but there was no such thing. My days were all rolled into one. It was like one giant stretch of nothing-doing. I would sit on the edge of the bed for hours—just sit, and stare, and not really think much of anything, not that I can recall. I had no appetite. I wouldn't talk to anyone. I wouldn't shower, for days and days, until Emme would drag me into the bathroom and scream at me to get under the spray, and at those times I wished I could melt away like the Wicked Witch of the West and slip down the drain.

When I was thinking clearly—or at least when I *thought* I was thinking clearly—I'd run through all the different ways I might take my life. Hanging. Carbon-monoxide poisoning. Pills. Slitting my wrists and bleeding out in the bathtub. For some reason, I never thought of slitting my neck, like my great-grandfather the cattle rustler, but that would have clearly done the trick. It was like some sick parlor game, only I was dead serious. Whatever desperate act

I'd seen in a movie or read about in a newspaper, I'd try it on and see if it fit. I even thought of those stupid Wile E. Coyote cartoons and wondered where I'd have to walk in New York City to increase my chances of getting hit by a falling safe. And that wasn't me with a sense of humor; that was me being practical. I kept getting caught up in the hit-or-miss aspects of suicide, in the thought that I might go through all these motions and still come up short. That to me was even worse than whatever I was going through. I hated the idea of taking a gun to my head and somehow misfiring, and walking around the rest of my life with my ear blown off, or driving recklessly enough to cause a crash and ending up merely paralyzed.

Still, I'd give every method some thought. For the longest time I fantasized about jumping off the George Washington Bridge, or crashing my car into a tree off the Palisades Parkway, but I was too chickenshit to pull it off. Sometimes, if I was feeling up to it, I'd go for a run in the mornings and catch myself leaning into oncoming traffic. There was no real shoulder on the side of the road, and I'd tease the temptation to jump out in front of every car that headed my way. I played all these little games in my head, ran through all these scenarios, but ultimately I couldn't see putting someone else in the middle of my suicide. Emme would find me in a bathtub filled with my blood and have to live with that image for the rest of her life. Or I'd jump in front of someone's car and that poor sucker would have to live with it for the rest of *his* life.

I laughed to myself at the irony in my thinking—after all, suicide is a supremely selfish act, and yet here I was, not so self-absorbed that I would take someone down with me, and not so far gone that I could no longer tell the difference between right and wrong.

I learned later that I used to write little notes to myself during this period—idle thoughts and to-do lists and fevered ramblings about this and that. Apparently I'd gotten in the habit of writing these notes the year before, when I was in the middle of a sudden and inexplicable dark period that would foreshadow my full-blown depression. For about a month or so, I was overwhelmingly tired, and I had difficulty getting out bed, and then, just as suddenly and inexplicably, the darkness lifted and my energy returned. It was the strangest thing. During that weird "down" time, I started writing these lists, or reminders . . . things I meant to accomplish when my outlook improved. In going over my notes for this book, I came across three yellow Post-its from my little predepression, with the following checklist:

Belief system.
Who you are, what have you done, where are you
   going?
Pain . . . own it.
Deal with issues at hand.
Project the future but don't obsess.
Don't be afraid to learn . . . focus.
Ask for help!
Take life lightly . . . that's why angels have wings.
Listen to your inner being.
Approach life with less stress.
Thank-you notes.
We are all human . . . be less judgmental.

Think before you speak.

Play guitar to my daughter.

Mind you, I have no recollection of actually *writing* these notes, but they turn up around the house, scribbled in a hand I can barely make out as my own, showing an outlook I no longer remember having. They're written on torn scraps of paper, or on square yellow Post-it notes, or left-behind legal pads.

As time passed and my depression began to take hold, the notes took on a far more ominous tone. "I am so uncomfortable in my body I could scream," I wrote in one of them, I guess after things had taken a turn for the considerably worse. "I don't know how long I can keep going. I want to die yet want to live. What shall I do?"

Emme tells me now that she used to find these notes, tucked away in my desk drawer or bookmarked into the pages of whatever hardcover happened to be lying around, and silently freak. It scared the crap out of her. She couldn't accept that the man she married was given to such dark thoughts, or that no one in our wide and supportive circle of friends was able to offer any substantive, proactive support. There was a lot of cheerleading, a lot of *Hey, hang in there!*–type sentiments, but nobody really understood depression. That was her biggest frustration, she says now. She felt so alone, because no one seemed to believe her when she said I was really in deep, serious, suicidal trouble. Even my doctors didn't think I was capable of taking my own life, but Emme knew different. She moved about expecting the worst, while all around everyone else was hoping for the best—and the hell of being married to me lay somewhere in between.

I was depressed. Clinically, and every which way besides. To the best of any doctor's professional judgment, it was a depression brought about by chronic pain—but at the same time it was a depression that might have been lurking, waiting for any old opportunity to show itself. That's how it goes with most mental illnesses. You can line up a whole bunch of doctors and every one of them will have a different theory or diagnosis, or a different explanation to justify a certain type of behavior, or a different course of treatment to set things right. In my case, there's a chance that even without the chronic pain the depression would have caught up to me sooner or later. There's a chance it might have been fueled by the genetic predisposition I wrote about earlier, and some folks I talked to thought it might have flowed in some way from the emotional upheaval that came after the September 11, 2001 terrorist attacks, which came just a month after the birth of our daughter, which came in the wake of a midlife career change that saw me managing a new phase in my wife's many-faceted career. There's a chance it had to do with the rapid decline of my courageous younger brother, Jonathan, who had battled brain cancer for going on sixteen years but who now appeared to be heading into his final months. There was a whole list of possible causes and explanations and mitigating stresses, and yet they all added up to one basic truth: I was a complete and total mess, and it would be nearly two years before a pharmacy of medications and a series of controversial electroconvulsive treatments began to set me right.

I hated life, although I don't ever think I hated me. It seems a fine point now, a small distinction, but at the time it was big as life. What I hated was not being able to *be* me, if that makes any sense. The old me. Full of life, and energy, and ready to rock 'n' roll. That me was way out of reach. That me was unrecognizable. It got to where I couldn't even see myself in the mirror. At five feet eleven, my normal weight was about 175 pounds, and I got down to 130 or so. I'd spend hours looking in the mirror, and I'd usually end up berating myself, and beating the crap out of myself. Literally. There'd be welts on my face from where I slapped myself. I would hard-punch the refrigerator, leaving dents in the door that still serve as reminders of those dark days every time I reach for something to eat. I would tug on my stomach and think I was fat, although in truth I was weak and frail and bone skinny. Another irony: I was married to a world-famous supermodel who lectured all over the country on body image and self-esteem, while I was thin as a rail and thinking I was fat. Where was the learned truth in *that*? Hell, I wasn't just married to Emme. I was managing her career as well, which meant I was out there spreading the same message, for all the good it did me.

There was room in my thinking for all kinds of weird, runaway thoughts. I thought of Dr. Wharton and all his other patients. I thought of Toby, and everything I was missing. I thought of my brother Jonathan and how I couldn't be there for him, or for anyone else in my family. Or my head would run to something mundane, like a shower, or television, or a piece of paper I might be determined to fill with indecipherable musings and doodlings. It's strange the way the human brain works—or, in my case, the way it sometimes doesn't. Why would anyone not want to shower for days and days? It makes no sense, but that was me; the depression left me doing things that made no sense and thinking they were the most natural thing in the world. I wouldn't shave, also for days and days. I wouldn't eat. And then, just like that, I'd overeat. There was no explaining it, except to say it was the depression. That was always the answer, to every bizarre behavior. *It's not me. It's the depression.* Sometimes it took me twenty minutes just to tie my shoes, and I remember being frustrated, nearly to tears, that I couldn't complete such a simple task. And the shower? Man, that was always an adventure. I used to stand underneath the spray until the hot water ran out, and then I'd stand under the cold spray for another ten, fifteen minutes. At some point, I'd get distracted and step out of the shower and dry off.

Everything was a chore, as you can see from the following journal entry:

Nov. 18, '02
Life is truly difficult. I have no appetite. I'm too sane to kill myself. It would be selfish. Hate food now. Eating is so difficult for me. I used to love to eat but now I don't. I'm spoiled and dumb. I need to feed Toby, but how? I can't feed myself. I need to walk, but I'm resisting myself. I have not checked my e-mail. Life is for the living. I'm dead inside!!!

Emme arranged it so I would occasionally have dinner at my parents' house, just a couple towns over from where we lived. I think she did this whenever she had a meeting or an event she needed to attend in the city—or maybe she just needed a break from time to time, and my parents were more than happy to have me over for dinner. At least, that's how I remember it. Emme tells me now that these dinners were not all that frequent, that I was at her side more often than not, and it was only a handful of times over these down months when she left me with my folks. In any case, she couldn't have picked a better, safer, or more nurturing place to park me than my parents' house. It was the same house I grew up in, but I couldn't drive there on my own. I couldn't find my way. How ironic is that? How creepy? But that's what depression can do to you; it can make you lose your moorings, and leave you feeling like you'll never get back to where you started.

Anyway, I used to sit at my parents' table, and my father would tell me, "One thing at a time." That was his mantra for breaking these huge steps down into small, manageable strides. *One thing at a time.* Like tying my shoes and taking a shower and feeding my daughter and writing a check were these great big deals. I ate very slowly, because I had no interest in food. And I barely spoke, because my mother would say that if I had nothing positive or constructive to say I should keep quiet. I couldn't blame her. I was the same broken record in my parents' house as I was at home with Emme, or in Dr. Wharton's office: *When will I get better? I'm going to kill myself. When will I get better? I'm going to kill myself* . . . Even I could see how this might get tiring after a while. I'm sure I put my parents through hell during those interminable dinners. Jonathan wasn't doing well, and his doctors were saying it would now be a matter of weeks or months for him, and my poor parents had to sit there and listen to me rattle on about taking my own life! Talk about bad timing—but, I guess, we can no sooner schedule our depressions than we can regulate our bad moods.

My mom used to pull me aside and try to reach me through the haze in my head. "Phil," she'd say, "please, you must get better. It's enough we're going to lose Jonathan. I won't survive if I lose you, too."

It's like she thought she could shake it out of me, that I could just snap out of it, or will myself whole, and I wanted to say, "Mom, believe me, I want to get better. I just can't figure out how!" And the thing of it is, my mother knew this as well as anybody, but all I could do was nod, or stare off into space, or mumble something incoherent that I'm sure she didn't find all that reassuring. I *was* doing my best, but even I could see that my best wasn't all that much.

Whatever strength I managed to find seemed to flow through Toby. It was an awful lot of power to invest in such a tiny little package, but she was almost perfectly suited to the role. Some mornings, when I couldn't seem to get myself up and out, sometimes stretching into afternoons and early evenings, I'd sit around the house, watching videos with her. She was big into this "Baby Einstein" series, and Emme would pop in a tape and leave us to do her thing. Toby had her favorite little chair, and I would sit next to her, and the two of us would be mesmerized by these videos. I had no idea what I was watching, but it was very much on my mind that I was *with* Toby. This was my way of being with her. I wouldn't say much. I *couldn't* say much. But we'd sit, and watch, and be together, and I found great comfort in that. There's a lot I seemed to miss, and a lot I've lost to my mental illness, but this is one piece that came through.

The penile pain was almost completely gone by the end of February 2003, although I didn't trust it at first. It went the way it came, which was pretty suddenly. It became manageable by early fall, to where I was finally able to function and focus, but by that point the depression had set in and it didn't much matter. I could sit still long enough to socialize, but I didn't have the head for it. I could sit still long enough to return some phone calls and some e-mail, but I didn't have the head for it. I could start experiencing life again, but I didn't have the head for it. And yet even once the pain had gone, I felt sure it would return. It was like waiting for the other shoe to drop. I kept waking up each morning, expecting agony. It was always in the back of my mind, the worry that it would come back and bite me again. I'd test it a lot, just to be sure. I'd do a Kegel-type exercise, where I'd stop the urine midstream while I was peeing, pulling in those muscles in my groin, and I marveled that it didn't hurt, but I didn't trust it. I didn't trust that the pain had finally gone and yet I was still in a depression. I thought, *Okay, now the pain's gone, so why can't I go back to the old Phil?* I couldn't understand that. Dr. Wharton explained that I'd had a major chemical imbalance, and that the brain is the organ in the body that takes the longest time to heal. He kept telling me that with exercise, proper medication and time I would eventually get out of my depression, but I didn't trust that either.

My sex drive still hadn't returned. I had no libido whatsoever. Emme and I hadn't made love in the longest time.

(She could probably tell you *exactly* how long it had been.) Emme had thought all along that once the pain disappeared from my prostate area we would be able to resume our healthy sex life, but that was the furthest thing from my mind. As hard as everything must have been for her, there was also that, but I didn't have the energy, or the drive. Still, we managed to make love once or twice, after the pain finally lifted. It's almost like I had to force myself to do it, and I ended up just sobbing in Emme's arms. I felt so helpless, so useless. I wondered if I would ever again be able to feel that sense of intimacy with the woman I loved, if those moments were now lost to me forever, and the real sadness was that it didn't strike me as such a tremendous loss. I cried for what I was costing Emme, for what might be lost to *her* forever, more than what I was costing me, or for what might be lost to me forever. I didn't care if I ever had sex again, but I cared deeply that Emme might never again know that closeness, that intimacy, that sense of release. The thought terrified me, and when I was in the mood to talk I used to tell Emme to go out and find someone else, someone who could be a real husband to her and a real father to Toby. And I was sincere about it. She deserved to be married to a man who desired her as completely as I used to. She deserved to be loved and lusted over and put on a pedestal. She deserved all these things, and a whole lot more, and I could no longer give them to her, which I took to mean that I no longer deserved her.

For her part, Toby deserved to have a father who could take care of her, who could do more than sit alongside her while she watched "Baby Einstein" videos. Toby deserved a father who would be present for the milestone moments of her growing up. My illness had left me wrong for both Emme and Toby, and I was okay with that—which, of course, was a whole other sadness.

Somehow, through all of this weirdness and darkness, Emme managed to shine these powerful rays of light on our little lives. It was the most incredible thing. Where she found the strength or the brave face, I'll never know, but she dug deep and pressed on. She was even able to throw me a surprise party for my fortieth birthday, at a local ice-skating arena. It was just family, and she threw it together with my sister-in-law, Liora, because of course it was Seth's fortieth birthday, too. They came up with some pretense to drag us down to the local ice-skating rink, and the real surprise was that they had arranged for Oksana Baiul, the great Ukrainian figure skater, to attend. (Emme had met Oksana through their mutual publicist.) I guess if you're going to throw a skating party, it makes sense to invite an Olympic gold medalist, right?

I look back and think what a courageous thing it was, to arrange a party during such a stressful time, but that was Emme for you. Check that: that was Emme for *me*. Really, she was so completely there for me during my depression, even when her patience flagged, even when I pushed all her buttons, even when I couldn't bring myself to make love with her, even when she was feeling lonely and helpless and like there was no way out of it. I don't know how I would have managed without her, and I think about all those poor, desperate souls who find themselves in a depression without the amazing love and support I got from Emme, and from my wonderful friends and family. How in the world do they get through it?

With Emme, there was always hope. She put a brave face on everything, and here she rolled the dice that I would be able to keep it together for at least this one evening, and that maybe the evening itself would pull me out of my funk, even for just a short while. And it did, for a precious few hours. I loved to skate. I didn't have my own skates with me so I couldn't skate the way I would have liked, but I skated just the same, and after a while I was really flying across that ice, doing these neat little half flips, waltz jumps, spins, and all these other cool moves that used to come so naturally. And do you know what? During those brief moments, out there on the ice, surrounded by people who loved me and who were rooting for me, I finally felt free. It was a pocket of hope and happiness, in the middle of all kinds of pain and confusion.

Nov. 20, '02

9 p.m. . . . West Wing, West Wing, West Wing. Emme loves West Wing. I'm anxious. Very out of it. I think I've gone mad. I can't write a check. Very scary. I'm going down.

Nov. 25, '02

Just got off the phone with Dr. Wharton. He told me to write in my journal . . . My physical pain that I hold back is mentally killing me. I have so much more than others, yet it's my "toe" that hurts. The day is young and so am I. I'm on hold and life is speeding away. It's moving. I need a full-time babysitter. I create things, and over and over in my head they play. They are not real.

No question, life was speeding away, and it just about killed me. Now that the penile pain had subsided, this was the most painful part, the dawning realization that my life was unfolding without me. As we turned the corner from Thanksgiving and headed into the year-end holidays, I reminded myself that I hadn't been myself for over a year, and it was almost as unbearable as the depression. Really, I lived for this time of year, and I'd already missed out on Toby's first Chanukah and Christmas, and now here I was, looking at missing her second set of holidays. Jonathan, too, was likely facing his last holiday season, and I was in no shape to embrace the bittersweetness of it with him. *I was missing everything!* You have to realize, Emme and I had been together for a good long time by this point—thirteen years!—so we had a chunk of history in reserve, but we had waited so long to start our little family, I kept thinking that our life together didn't really start until Toby came along. However I looked at it, the times of my life were passing me by, and the depression was robbing me of all these precious moments, and it didn't matter what medications I took, or how many therapy sessions I endured, or where I turned for support or guidance . . . I was powerless against it.

The Other Side of Patience

I was the strong devoted wife for about a year and a half. Smiling and running the household. Putting up a good front at the office. Making apologies for Phil. Taking frontline care of Toby. Coordinating our schedules and doctor appointments with our babysitter. Picking up all the pieces and trying to make a good go of things, all things considered. Eighteen months, and that was about all I could handle, and I look back on that period now and wonder how I kept up such a good front for so long.

Really, it takes a lot out of you, caring for someone in a depression, especially with a toddler underfoot. It's like being a single parent ten times over, because there's the baby to take care of, and on top of that there's your partner, and there can be such wild, unpredictable mood swings that you never know what to expect. And there's no letup. Most new parents, they give each other some downtime while they take turns caring for the baby. Or they put the baby down for the night, and they can at least spend some quality alone time together, or unwind with a glass of wine or a good book, but we didn't have any of that. There was always some new crisis or agony to get past. There was no sense that we were in this thing together. Phil was off by himself, battling his demons, struggling through his illness in whatever ways he could, and I was off in caregiver mode, doing what I needed to do to keep him reasonably safe and well-fed and nurtured enough to find room to get better, all the while looking after Toby.

I should mention here that Toby was (and remains!) an unusual child. She was a godsend. I write about her now as a source of sweetness and light and hope, and I know it comes across as a mother's wishful or wistful thinking, but that's really how she was. Yes, taking care of an infant child is tough, tiring work, especially for a single parent, but Toby never gave me any kind of hard time. Not once. In fact, she so rarely cried that I took her to the pediatrician one afternoon to make sure there was nothing wrong with her. I mean, what kind of toddler never cries? She never even fussed, so I assumed there was something horrible going on inside her little head, but her doctor assured me that Toby was completely normal. She just had one of those easygoing dispositions, and it's a good thing, too, because I don't know how I would have handled it if she was like "most" other babies in this department.

I should mention also that I received enormous support from knowledgeable friends and family members—and that I'm sure I took enormous advantage of these relationships

throughout our ordeal. In particular, our friends Marc Snow-
man and Dr. Jane Greer, both therapists, were endlessly
helpful, and Dr. Alex Hoffer, Seth's father-in-law, was always available—not just to me, but to Phil as well. When I
tell people to use your contacts, I mean it. I called these good
people no matter the time, day or night, and no matter the
question, big or small, and they were always there for us.

In the beginning, I got through it thinking all Phil
needed was some time, and some rest, and a big, cheerful
smile from me and Toby, and eventually he'd be okay. But
my smile faded as his depression dragged on, and as our
wide circle of friends began to shrink. Don't get me wrong:
we were surrounded by wonderful friends and family, but
unless you had a frame of reference for this sort of thing,
unless you had some sort of Aronson-cam mounted in
strategic spots around our house, it was impossible to have
a clear sense what Phil was going through, what *we* were
going through. It's like I had to give some of our friends instructions on how to act around Phil, almost to where I had
to write them a script for how each visit would go. Everyone wanted to help, but they didn't quite know how, and as
the depression lingered we saw fewer and fewer people. I
guess we weren't easy to be around, and I understood that.
Plus, people had their own busy lives and their own problems to deal with. I understood that, too, even as our busy
lives and our problems began to close in around us.

Seth knew the deal, but we didn't always agree on what
was best for Phil. We both wanted him to get better, and
soon, but I guess we had different approaches and perspec-
tives. Seth remembered how things had been for him, back

when he was in his depression, and naturally assumed that Phil's illness would follow the same course, but everyone's different. Every depression is different. What works in some cases doesn't work at all in others. The one piece they had in common, though, was the way each of them craved sleep. Seth told me that was the only thing he could do that would give him any kind of relief, and Phil was clearly on the same page. He just wouldn't get out of bed. If it had been up to him, he'd have spent months in bed. Each day, it was harder and harder to get him up and moving, and I was torn between letting him get the peace and quiet he needed and forcing him to experience life. Dr. Wharton felt strongly that Phil needed the stimulation of getting out of the house and interacting with other people, and some type of physical activity, so there was always a balance. I couldn't let Phil wallow in the sheets all day, so I had to be the bad guy on this—and I *hated* being the bad guy.

(Really, it was so counter to my personality that I didn't recognize myself. I'd hear myself taking a firm tone with Phil, or sounding like a drill sergeant, and think, *Who in the world is that?*)

At some point, when we were in the middle of Phil's depression, I started to think of my mom, and what she went through. She was diagnosed with lung cancer when she was only thirty-eight years old. I was fifteen. By the time they caught it, the cancer had spread to where it was only a matter of time, and yet in the short time she had left she managed to do some pretty amazing things—and most amazing of all was how she kept it together for her family. I was mostly out of the house, away at prep school, but she continued to take care of my stepfather, Bill, my brother, Chip, and my sister, Melanie. She continued to run the household. I don't know where she found the strength—not just the physical strength, mind you, but the emotional strength—and I did what I could to call on some measure of the same strength for me and my family. I wanted to channel some of that strength to help me deal with what was going on with Phil. It had only been months, and I was already drained. I wondered where people came up with the focus and intensity to cope with something like this. I thought maybe I'd missed a meeting, or some instruction manual that told caregivers how to muster a positive attitude, because I found myself feeling completely lost.

The real troubling shift for me was my loss of patience. Again, this was *so* not like me, but I became more and more short-tempered as Phil slipped deeper and deeper into depression. He used to tell me all the time that he couldn't stand living, that he was going to kill himself. I think it started just as something to say, or just some way to describe the pain he was in when the chronic pain was at its most intense, but after a while it seemed like he was talking about killing himself six, seven, eight times a day. Some days it was all he could talk about. It was like a fixation. He went from being vague about it to saying things like "Emme, I want you to move on if I'm not here. I want you to find another man and have pleasure with him and let him be a good father to Toby." At one point, he even started talking about how he wanted to be cremated. Obviously, as husband and wife, we'd talked about this type of thing before, from a rational, mentally healthy, estate-planning place, and I had never, ever heard this from him. From me, yes, but Phil was always clear that he wanted to be buried in a family plot. Now he was saying he didn't want the maggots eating at his body, and he didn't want to rot away in the dirt, and all kinds of graphic, ghoulish stuff, and it was such a huge departure from his usual point of view.

I just couldn't hear it. I couldn't stop Phil's runaway thoughts, but I didn't have to listen to them, and I thought I could at least keep him from running off his mouth. I could try to get him to talk about something else. I'd say, "Stop talking about killing yourself, Phil. If you don't stop talking about it, *I'm* going to kill you." I'd try to make a joke out of it, but it wasn't funny. I was serious, and so was he, but still I was ready to throttle him. Whatever patience I'd had going into this thing was long gone, and along with it went my good cheer and positive outlook. It just beat me down. I saw what thick shit we were in, and that there was no way out of it. That's how it left me thinking, that no matter what we did, no matter what medications Phil tried or what doctors we consulted, he wasn't getting better. It didn't matter that Dr. Wharton had explained to me that Phil's treatment would take time. It didn't matter that it had only been a few months and that we'd yet to stumble across the right combinations of medication and treatment. It didn't matter that all the research showed that many people in a depression eventually emerge from that depression, with the proper care. I didn't know if I could hold out that long, or how to know for certain that Phil was in fact getting the proper care. I didn't know a damn thing, beyond the blood-curdling truth that many people in a depression *did* succeed in killing themselves. It happened every day, and here I was, doing everything in my power to see that it didn't happen on this day, or the next day, or the one after that.

That second holiday season was particularly rough, for a slew of reasons. We had a bunch of people over to the house for Thanksgiving. Phil's entire family. My entire family. Friends. About thirty people in all. The house smelled wonderfully like pine, and there were two fireplaces going, and friends and neighbors dropping in all weekend long. Our house was always a warm, welcoming place, and we loved to entertain, so I found myself looking forward to the holiday, even though Phil clearly wasn't up to it. (There were no turkey-carving honors for him that year, I'm sad to report, for obvious reasons of Phil preservation.) At first, I had no idea whether he'd come out of our bedroom and make an appearance, but I pressed on and hoped for the best, and as it happened he did manage to engage. He was even the life of the party, for a stretch. Seth encouraged him to get out his guitar, and before long everyone was singing, and there was a warm glow of cheer and hopefulness and all those good things.

Phil always had a special aura about him whenever he played the guitar. The music seemed to light him up from the inside, and carry him to some special place, and that's how it was here. Let me tell you, it was a truly wonderful thing, to see him so transformed and transported. He's got a great singing voice, and it was incredibly nourishing to hear him sounding so lighthearted and high-spirited. It was almost like he was his old self again, for just those few moments, singing. James Taylor. Crosby, Stills, Nash & Young.

Cat Stevens. The Eagles. All these great songs he always used to play. And then, when the music stopped and the people disappeared, the light switched off and he was back to being down and hangdog and lethargic. His talk once again turned to monosyllabic grunts, as if the effort to string more than a couple words together was too great. It was such an abrupt, dramatic change, like someone had pulled a plug, and it made me incredibly angry at the time because I remember thinking it was something Phil could control. That was how it looked, from my outside perspective, like he could turn his moods off and on with a whim, from dark to light and back again, even though I knew full well that he couldn't control his illness any more than he could have controlled his chronic pain or his afib, but I was so frazzled and fragile by this point that when I saw him slip so easily into that other mode it had me a little confused.

For a couple weeks there, I labored under the misconception that Phil *could* turn things on and off, if he chose to do so, and with that mind-set I pretty much forced him out of the house to accompany me to a few Christmas parties. We had always been a very social couple, and a lot of that socializing was common to our business. People in modeling and fashion and television and advertising were always networking at parties, and there was a certain pressure to stay in the loop. But if I arranged to have people over for dinner, Phil would find reasons to squirrel himself away in our bedroom. If I dragged him to a Christmas party, I'd find him in the host's kitchen, with his back against the far corner of the wall, almost like he was willing himself through the boundaries of the party and into the open night air. It was all too much for him, he'd tell me later, and each time we left the house he longed to return home and jump under the covers and get back to his own little world. That was where he felt safe.

Anyway, I was a little slower than I should have been reading Phil's signals, and I'm still not sure whether it was a good move, but I kept pulling him back into our old life, willing him through all these familiar paces in hopes that he might fall back into step. For example, just after the new year, we stole away to St. Barths with close friends and family for my best friend's fortieth birthday vacation. I imagine a lot of folks might read this and think, *What's the deal with these people, taking vacations and going to parties and having people over for dinner during something as traumatic as a depression?* I'd probably think the same, but when we were in the middle of it I thought it was essential to keep up our normal routines, and to try to give Phil an opportunity to get outside this safe little world he was determined to make for himself, and our doctors agreed. It was February 2003, and I didn't know it at the time, but Phil was starting to experiment with his meds, taking himself off this or that drug or monkeying with his doses or restarting a medication that his doctors had discontinued. Whatever he was doing, the scary thing is that it appeared to have a positive effect on him. He had energy, and an appetite, and he seemed to take a genuine interest in what was going on around him. Although Phil was still struggling, it was a delicious few days for me. Phil did manage to run on the beach and work out a little bit. He'd lost a tremendous amount of weight— forty pounds or so—and started to put some of it back on.

Toby had a blast, playing in the surf and the sand. The weather was great, and the sun was calming, especially coming from the dead of a New Jersey winter, and my only regrets about the trip were that we didn't stay longer or take more pictures. This lack of photos might sound like a funny thing to regret, but once we got home I realized I needed the pictures to help spur Phil's memory. His brain still wasn't firing on all cylinders, and he was experiencing a great deal of memory loss. I'm sure the medication contributed to that, but even now, over two years later, and after more than a year of good-as-newness, Phil still can't recall a lot of what happened. That trip to St. Barths is mostly lost to him, and that's a shame, because it was a beautiful point of pause for us.

And the pictures weren't just for Phil. I think I needed them just as much back then, for the way they reminded me how we once were together, how we could be again. I look at those too-few pictures now and think of those too-few days as a sign—not that he was getting better, mind you, but that he was still fighting and struggling underneath the haze of all those meds. He was still Phil, deep down. He was still the man I married, the man I loved, the man I ached (literally!) to have him hold me in his arms each night in bed. The signs of his depression remained everywhere apparent. He continued to hang back in certain social situations, although he did take out his guitar from time to time. (He even wrote a couple new songs!) He was not all that talkative, and I suppose I still felt like I was "husband-sitting," but the change of scenery did us enormous good. And of course, on a very surface level at least, Toby and I really had a break from what was turning out to be a dark and gloomy winter back home.

We headed back to Jersey and faced whatever lay in wait. Truth be told, there were a lot of difficult moments in the year ahead, but they're mostly a blur. In Phil's case, a lot of this stuff just didn't register, or if it did it only made a brief impression. In my case, I've chosen to blot out a lot of what happened because it was so painful, and I guess I didn't want to have to live through it all again in memory. In any case, once it became clear that I couldn't leave Phil alone, and that I had to stay on top of him with his medications, and that our baseline measure for Phil's well-being was headed lower still, time just seemed to tick away with nothing to mark its passing. Looking back, I can make out a long stretch of days without a whole lot going on to distinguish one from the next. There were moments when Phil seemed to be doing a bit better, but they were always quickly followed by moments when it was clear he was still struggling. There was also a frightening stretch of weeks when Phil's self-medicating experiment seemed to really take hold. He got it in his head that he could do a better job of it than Dr. Wharton. There was one night in particular when it seemed the old Phil was back. He had just taken his evening meds, and I naturally assumed he had taken the prescribed cocktail, but at about ten o'clock he started talking a blue streak. I hadn't heard him string so many words together in weeks and weeks. He started telling me about his dreams, about his visions for our future, about how much better he was feeling. He said, "Oh my God, Emme. I think I'm really getting better."

I wanted desperately to believe him, but there was

something *off* about this transformation in his behavior. He was wild, almost manic—closer to the old Phil than I'd seen in a while, but almost like he was a Phil from some alternate universe. Like a turbo-Phil, a fun-house Phil. Still, I played along, enjoying having some semblance of my husband back. It lasted for about an hour, and he was all over the place, talking about anything and everything and actually making sense. If I closed my eyes and tried really hard I could almost imagine we were back to normal, although at that point I was so desperate for his company I would have taken any reasonable facsimile and accepted it as Phil.

After about an hour, Phil crashed, and by the next morning he was back once again in one of his low, down states. Like he'd been for the past months. Hardly saying anything. Hardly remembering anything from the night before. Hardly moving a muscle unless I was tugging him out of bed. Who knows? He might have even been a little worse off than he had been before this curious little window opened up for us, if such a thing was possible.

I said, "Phil, do you remember those things you were saying to me last night, about how much better you were feeling?" And he just looked at me like he didn't have the slightest idea what I was talking about.

That night, again about nine thirty, ten o'clock, the old Phil came back for another visit. He'd been playing with his medications again, and I guess he stumbled on this little side benefit. He was wired, like he'd been the night before, and far more talkative than he'd been, and apparently clearheaded—still a little *off*, but a lot closer to *on* than I'd seen in a while.

Whatever it was that had caused the change, I thought it was a product of the *proper* medications, and I welcomed it. I said, "Phil, I've missed you so much. I haven't been able to talk to you."

He said, "Em, I've missed you too. It's been a nightmare. But I'm getting better now. I can feel it. We're going to be fine."

I said, "Are you sure?"

He said, "I promise." And then he held me—my sick shell of a husband actually reached out to comfort *me*—and assured me that everything was going to be okay. I was so happy, and so eager to believe he was truly getting better, I cried. Phil cried, too, and then, about an hour into this tiny reprieve, he crashed. Same way he'd done the night before. He was up, high, and then he was down, hard. It was the craziest thing, but I talked myself into believing that he was getting better, that it made some kind of twisted sense for the depression to disappear from the nighttime backward, that each night going forward I'd have more and more time with the old Phil, until pretty soon those reprieves would become his baseline level and lasted the entire day and he was whole once again. Anyway, that's how he had me thinking, and things went on in this way for another few nights—each time as a result of his self-medicating. Whatever he was doing, he was getting this chemically induced high late at night, and riding it into thinking it was a sign that he was nearly cured.

After three nights, he said, "Emme, I've got to tell someone about this." Then he raced upstairs to our office and started making phone calls. It was late, ten thirty or so, but he made six or seven calls. Mostly he got a bunch of answering machines, and he left messages like "I'm letting you know this is all behind me." "Tonight is a turning point in my life." "The nightmare is over."

I listened in and wanted to tell him to take it a little slower, to give it some time to see if these pockets of "normal" got any longer or more certain, but he was on this weird roll, and he was so excited. He just had to keep calling, and talking, and convincing everyone that he was finally better, which of course gave him the opportunity to talk himself into it as well.

Naturally, he crashed soon after, and the next morning I was devastated all over again when I couldn't get him out of bed and he was in his same baseline state, and I went with him to his next appointment with Dr. Wharton to make sure he talked about it. As much as I loved these little visits from fun-house Phil, I worried they were some kind of warning sign.

Sure enough, Phil had been playing with his Ambien, doubling up on his dosage—not because he was making any kind of honest mistake, but because he thought maybe he'd get a better response trying it his way for a while. It's a sleep medication, and he was always having trouble sleeping, so I guess he was trying to up his chances. And it wasn't just the Ambien. He was playing around with a lot of his dosages, skipping this one, halving that one, doubling up on that other one . . . all of which made it impossible for Dr. Wharton to accurately track his progress, and left me feeling like I'd been banging my head against the wall for the past half year or so, trying to get this thing under control.

At around this time, I encouraged Phil to seek out another doctor to complement Dr. Wharton's treatment. Phil's family had great confidence in Dr. Wharton, and rightly so, but after all these months I started to feel that Phil wasn't getting where we wanted him to be, at least not quickly enough, so I felt there ought to be another voice, another perspective in the mix. I also felt that a woman's point of view was sorely needed in our treatment plan—not least because it sometimes seemed as if *I* was having as much trouble dealing with Phil's depression as Phil. We ended up in the care of Dr. Nomita Sonty, from the Pain Management Center at Columbia Presbyterian, where Dr. Wharton was also affiliated. Dr. Sonty was a very nice woman, with a methodology that was somewhat different from Dr. Wharton's. She was straightforward, and to the point. She took a real proactive approach, and Phil seemed to respond well to her. Dr. Sonty encouraged him to attend the group therapy sessions that were run at the hospital, to examine what he was going through up against what some other patients were experiencing with their depressions.

Phil didn't really get the kind of benefit out of group that we'd hoped he might, but he made a good go of it. He went through the motions, at least, although whenever I asked him about these sessions afterward he'd kind of shrug his shoulders, as if to suggest they weren't all that helpful. He reminded me of a kid coming home from school, when his parents ask how his day went, and all he can say is "Fine." Or the parents ask what he did, and all they'd get back is "Nothing." I think Phil was there in body but not in spirit. He's since told me that he couldn't stand to listen to other people talk about their troubles. It's not that he wasn't a compassionate soul, because he's always been quick to lend an ear or a hand to someone in need, but in this case he just couldn't see that he had anything in common with these other patients. They were barking up entirely different trees, as far as Phil was concerned, I guess because he hadn't reached that "rock bottom" place in his depression to recognize that they were all essentially in the same place. And so he would listen to people share their stories, but he wouldn't *listen*. He couldn't concentrate, or contribute, because in his mind there was no connection between his experiences and the experiences of everyone else in the room. God knows, it was hard enough for him to keep his own story straight in his head, so how could we expect him to follow the ups and downs of complete strangers?

Also around this time, I started feeling a little down and dark and depressed myself, so I tried to carve out some time for myself away from Phil. It's a wearying thing, to be surrounded by all these dark thoughts on such a constant basis. I felt it was important for me and Toby to get a little distance from Phil—and for Phil to get a little distance from us. Trouble was, Phil couldn't be left alone, so I called up my mother-in-law one day and told her I needed her to look after Phil for a while. I knew it was a bad time for her, and that she had her hands full with Jonathan, but I was at a kind of breaking point. I'd arranged to drive up to Massachusetts to see our dear family friends the Carles, to recharge and refresh. I didn't tell Phil what I was up to right off the bat; I just quietly packed some of his things and told him we were going to his parents' house for a visit. Judy wasn't sure if he was coming over for dinner or for a couple nights—and, frankly, neither was I. The only thing I was sure about was that I needed to get away with Toby, to put some distance between me and Phil's depression so I could get a little perspective on it, and a little relief, but by the time we pulled into his old driveway Phil could tell something was up.

He said, "What are you doing?"

I said, "I need to drop you off at your mom's for a bit. I can't leave you alone, and I need to not be around you." I was nice enough about it, but I suppose there's no *nice* way to deliver that kind of message.

He said, "Where are you going?"

I said, "Up to Massachusetts for a short visit, to see Eric and Bobbie. I need to get away."

He started talking his usual nonsense, about killing himself, and me moving on and finding someone else, and I tried to shut him up. I said, "That's enough, Phil. I don't want to hear you talking about not being here. I don't want to hear you talking about me being with other men. I love you dearly, and I know you love me, and we will get back to how we were. I promise."

At just that moment, I wasn't sure it was a promise I could keep, but I needed to say something, and I needed it to be positive, and I needed to disengage. Of course, nothing would have made me happier than to get back to how we were, but I didn't know how to get there from here. I didn't know what buttons to push to help us past this tough patch.

I've got to tell you, leaving Phil at his parents' house that day was one of the hardest things I ever had to do. It was one of the real low points of his depression for me, right down there with finding him nearly unconscious the morning he tried to take his life. It felt like I was abandoning him, even though I knew I needed a little respite. Phil too must have felt abandoned, and alone, even though he was with his parents, because he bolted. He ran away from his parents' house before I even had a chance to pull out of the driveway, and for an agonizing hour or so nobody could find him.

Here's how it went down: I was in the driver's seat, getting ready to pull away from the house, when my cell phone started to ring. It was Phil. I thought, *Hmmm, that's strange.* He said, "You don't have to worry about me anymore, Em."

I assumed Phil was calling me from inside his parents' house, and didn't read too much into the call beyond it being a bizarre way to say another good-bye. "I'll always worry about you, Phil," I said, "just like you'll always worry about me."

"No," he said, "I mean you won't have to worry about having me babysat anymore."

Just then, Phil's parents noticed the back door to the house had been flung open, and they couldn't find Phil anywhere inside the house. I was still in the driveway, still on the phone with Phil, still unaware that anything else was going on, but within seconds my in-laws were upon me, telling me that Phil had disappeared. Phil must have heard the commotion on my end of the phone, because he cut the call. It was the most incongruous thing. In a million years, it never would have occurred to me that Phil would bolt from his parents' house, but he was gone. I got out of the car and ran around the outside of the house for a bit, half expecting to find him behind a tree or something. Also, I immediately tried him back on his cell phone, but he wouldn't answer. My father-in-law started driving around the neighborhood on a frantic search—and, as it turned out, he didn't have to look too long or too far. He found Phil a short time later, hanging on the swing set at his elementary school playground a couple blocks away, lost in some daydream from childhood, or remembering what it was like to be young and carefree and not burdened by depression. As relieved as my father-in-law must have been to have found Phil, it must have also been heart wrecking, to see him so lost and forlorn and out of it, but at least he knew that Phil was safe.

It was one of the weirdest, most troubling episodes of Phil's depression to date, but it wasn't enough to keep me from my plans. I'd reached some kind of breaking point. I told Phil I needed to get away. I told him it would only be for a couple days. Phil promised me he wouldn't disappear like that, and I took him at his word. It's like I didn't have any choice.

And so, less than two hours after his disappearing act, I was headed north. I was completely empty, but I knew I could get my cup filled at the Carles'. There'd be good food, and peace and quiet, and time to rejuvenate and refresh. Still, I cried the whole way up Route 91 to Massachusetts. Really, the tears just streamed down my face. Toby was sleeping peacefully in the backseat, and I was bawling like a baby, and I don't think I stopped crying until I arrived.

Playing to Lose

PHIL

I hated group therapy. It was hard enough dealing with my own suicidal thoughts without having to make sense of anyone else's. Plus, I wasn't exactly the most social animal at the time, and the idea of spending all those hours with a group of complete (and, completely depressed) strangers wasn't all that high on my list of preferred activities. I had no idea what to expect, but I wasn't expecting much. It was set up like every group therapy scene I'd ever seen in the movies, but the difference was that everyone talked and talked and talked. In the movies they edit out everything but the good stuff, so I wasn't prepared for all the talking and my mind kind of wandered as we worked our way around the room. When it came around to me I don't think I gave a very thorough presentation. I kept pretty much to the surface. I said things like "I don't feel like doing much of anything." Or, my "greatest hit"—"I want to kill myself."

And I didn't pay a whole lot of attention to whatever came my way in response.

But Emme and Dr. Sonty insisted I make the effort, and Dr. Wharton agreed, so I went—for a while, anyway. It wasn't always easy to muster up the strength to keep my appointments, but they loomed on my calendar like the only thing worth doing in my entire week, so how could I *not* go? A lot of times I went by myself. The routine, for a while, was for me to ride my bike across the George Washington Bridge from New Jersey, because I kind of freaked Emme out with all my talk about driving my car headlong into a tree, or oncoming traffic, or off one of the cliffs of the Palisades. As Emme wrote earlier, driving was out of the question once I told her that I'd driven Toby to one of her little music classes and had no recollection of how I'd gotten there, or how we'd gotten home. Emme was vigilant, but I don't think she realized how gone I was in this regard. It was pretty scary. Clearly, I should not have had access to a vehicle. One of my scary behaviors, early on, was to take my car out on the Palisades Parkway, and get it cranking, and then close my eyes. I drive a red 1994 Alfa Romeo Spider convertible—license plate 2RAN2LA (get it?)—and it's one of my favorite toys, but back then it was a lethal weapon. Back then it was my ride out of my depression—and it's a wonder I didn't wipe out a whole bunch of people along the way. I'd take the top down, get the car up to eighty, ninety miles per hour in nothing flat, and I'd be thinking, *Okay, here we go.* It would be the middle of the afternoon, the roads would be pretty clear, and I'd catch my reflection in the rectangle of the rearview mirror and just stare and stare. Then

I'd close my eyes, and open them, and close them, and open them.

It was like a giant game of chicken, and the stakes were life and death, and I was playing to lose.

I didn't recognize myself, staring back through the rearview on those death-defying rides up and down the Palisades. More than that, I didn't recognize my own impulses. I was some other person—a crazed, wild man!—on a winding road to self-destruction. It was like a challenge, to see how long I could keep my eyes closed before I found some reason to open them, all the while driving at speeds over a hundred miles an hour, sometimes up to one twenty. You have to realize, I'd never been one of those thrill-seeking speed demons on the open road, and I never got off on the exhilaration of pulling stupid stunts, but this was something else. This wasn't me pretending to be Jeff Gordon. This wasn't thrilling. This wasn't exhilarating. And it certainly wasn't a stupid stunt. This was merely a means to an end. This was me looking for the only way out. This was me bent on self-destruction. It got to where I'd close my eyes for six-, seven-, eight-second intervals, maybe longer. That's a long time to be driving at such reckless speeds with your eyes closed, I realize now, but at the time I kept thinking it wasn't enough time to do the trick. I guess I didn't have the willpower to keep them closed indefinitely, or maybe it was my survival instinct kicking in and forcing my eyes back open before it was too late, or maybe it was just a reflex. Whatever it was, each time I'd reopen my eyes, I'd notice a tree, or an overlook, and pray that I could close my eyes again and drive right into it.

I'd take off my seat belt. I wanted to be ejected from the car. That was the idea, to hit one of those trees at a hundred miles per hour and be thrown fifty feet into the air. I was thinking and not thinking both. I could picture the scene in my head, and there was room in my racing imagination for every possible outcome. The good outcome was that I would crash into a tree and be killed instantly. The bad outcome was that I would hit another car, and take out an innocent driver, or leave someone with a lifetime of guilt for colliding with me—even though, of course, it would have been my fault entirely. And then there were all the outcomes in between: I'd be tossed from the car and my clothes would snag on a branch of a tree; or I'd cause some other driver to swerve out of my way and *he'd* be the one who ended up wrapped around a tree; or I'd be left dangling fifty feet in the air, looking like an idiot; or I'd miss the mark and have to settle for a pair of broken legs and a couple of cracked ribs. I was so desperate to kill myself that even a violent end like the one I was imagining on that parkway would have been a relief. I should mention here that this driving-with-my-eyes-closed business happened more than once—it was a regular thing, for a while—but there must have been a part of my brain that registered the twists and turns of the road when my eyes were open and kept me driving on the asphalt when my eyes were closed, because I'm still here. By some miracle, I'm still here.

Even on my bicycle, though, I was a threat to do myself harm. I had always been big into cycling, and keeping fit, and I tried to keep that going when I was in my depression. It was all I had. The fifteen-mile ride into Manhattan would be my exercise for the day—a thirty-mile round-trip, which was a reasonable workout. On days when I had a doctor's appointment in the city, when the weather was decent, I'd tell myself I wouldn't have to go for a run, or go to the gym; I'd just ride back and forth to the city and that would be enough. I ride this really great Trek mountain bike—another favorite toy. It's heavy, with thick tires, and I've got all the accessories. The bike pants. The toe clips. The helmet. That's another one of the great ironies of my depression, that I'd set off on my bike, thinking of ways to kill myself, and still stop to put on my helmet.

A couple times, headed into the city to go to group, or to see Dr. Wharton or Dr. Sonty, I pulled up on the expanse of the George Washington Bridge, hopped off my bike, and caught myself staring down to the waters of the Hudson below. It was a god-awful long way down. You don't notice it when you're taking in the city skyline, or looking at the bridge from a distance, or even driving the span when you're in your car, but you're up there pretty high. I tried to calculate what it would be like to climb on top of the bridge railing and hurl myself into the water, and then to figure if I had the guts to pull it off. I leaned pretty far over the rail and tried to will myself into the water. I wonder now what all these passing motorists must have thought, driving by this decked-out cycling enthusiast, leaning precariously over the railing, if it even registered as something to think about. I was on a pedestrian and cycling path, running along the edge of the bridge, so it wasn't so unusual for drivers to see someone stopping for a rest or to take in the view. I never got so far as to swing my legs over the rail or anything like that, but I leaned pretty far over, for the longest time. It could have been a half hour or so before I'd climb back on my bike and continue my ride, and here again my thoughts were vivid and precise. My goal was clear. I could close my eyes and picture exactly what it would look like, me going over that railing, taking a header into the Hudson, but by some separate miracle I never saw it through.

It took until about February or so for the penile pain to completely lift, although the depression had long ago supplanted the pain as my killing worry.

Jan. 5, '03

I am hanging in. I have good days and bad days. The burning just doesn't want to let up and it can really drive you crazy. It has! I'm doing the best I can with it, though. God is helping me through this. So are my friends and relatives. I know there is a light at the end of the tunnel. It's dim but it's there.

My father had this great old saying: "Knock me down, but don't count me out." For the longest time, I embraced it as a motto to live by, but I reached a point where I'd been knocked down so many times that I wanted desperately to be counted out. There was no fight in me anymore. I was done. And yet there was always something to pull me back and get me to continue on my way, even as there was no way to keep me safe from my thoughts. Whenever I dodged one bullet, I immediately replaced it with another—that is, with a better, more efficient way out of my suffering. For some reason, I seemed to like to talk about all the different ways I might kill myself. I've since met folks who kept these types of thoughts to themselves, but I didn't spare Emme a single detail. I told her all my suicidal thoughts—to keep her close, to download my fevered imaginings, and maybe even to lash out at the fact that she was healthy and "enjoying life" while I was miserably and endlessly contemplating my own death. Predictably, as soon as I shared these moments on the bridge, my bicycle riding privileges were revoked, and Emme had to start driving me into the city for my appointments. Maybe that was my self-preservation instinct at work, because I'm sure I knew deep down that if I confessed these thoughts to Emme she would do everything she could to keep me safe, and I clearly didn't trust myself to keep me safe, so I left it to her. That's one way to look at it.

Ultimately, though, Emme couldn't save me from myself. She could take away my car keys and my bicycle, and she could leave me at my parents' house if she needed someone to "babysit" me for a couple hours, but I still had a certain amount of autonomy, and there was always another way out. More and more, that's how I started to think of it, whenever my thoughts ran to killing myself, which by the spring of 2003 was pretty much all the time. It was a way out, a way past the pain and anguish of depression. It's like you'd pull the plug on a machine if it was making too much noise; you'd kill the current, and the noise would stop, although with a machine you could always put the plug back in and get the thing started again. When the anxiety was at its worst, it felt as if a wild tiger was about to maul me, and these suicidal thoughts were my battle plans. They weren't cries for help. My cries for help were more straightforward. I'd look at Emme and say, "Em, you've got to help me!" Or I'd look to Seth for some strength or insight. No, this was me helping myself. This was me thinking what I could do to get past the pain, to outrun the wild tigers getting ready to maul me in my head.

It sounds a little bit like a contradiction, but this too was my survival instinct. That was very much part of my thought process at the time, that the only way to get past the depression, to survive the depression, was to kill myself. That's how bad it was. The thing of it is, I never *really* wanted to kill myself—at least not in the melodramatic, cheap-movie sense of the phrase. Oh, I was clearly suicidal, but it's like I had no choice. It was the depression; it wasn't me. The depression wanted to kill itself. It might seem like a fine point, but the distinction is everything. That's how it is with mental illness. Anyway, that's how it was with me. If I had to undergo chemotherapy to be treated for cancer, the radiation would kill my healthy cells alongside the cancerous cells. It poisons your whole body. It's the same with a depression. It takes your every waking moment and fills it with these noxious thoughts that color absolutely everything about you. It's impossible to look at any aspect of your life—work, relationships, hobbies, interests—in any kind of healthy way, because that healthy perspective has been compromised. Yes, it was a combustible mix: the depression wanted to kill itself, and at the same time I wanted to save myself from my depression.

I couldn't chase these thoughts for trying. They followed me all over town—and with them came a whole bunch of others. I kept thinking of my good buddy Dave. Seth and I used to hang with him all through high school. We were all really close. Dave was actually a great help to us when Seth was in his depression. He'd come over and drag Seth out for a run, or keep him connected to our former classmates with interesting local stories, or try to distract him with an outing or activity of some kind. Sometimes, the three of us would go running at the track, and whenever we did it was like we were back in high school all over again; we all had our busy lives and our separate shit to deal with, but for an hour or so we were teenagers again, running free. When Seth and I moved out of our parents' house and into our own two-bedroom condo in Leonia, New Jersey, Dave kept coming out and taking us for runs, although at some point our runs became less and less frequent, and soon enough there were months and months when we wouldn't see each other. Still, there was always a closeness among the three of us, a special bond, which is why it took me and Seth so completely by surprise when we learned Dave had taken a bunch of pills and killed himself—August 22, 1995. His mother told us afterward that he had gotten really paranoid, and really depressed, and we'd had no idea he was suffering. He'd been so present for Seth, and yet he couldn't reach out and let Seth do the same for him.

We went to Dave's wake, and I saw him lying there in his coffin. It was the first time I'd ever seen a dead body at a wake, and I don't think I handled it all that well. I wanted to go over and shake him awake and say, "Dave, what the fuck are you doing? Let's get out of here and go for a run." But there's no getting out of here and going for a run, not after you swallow a fistful of pills, not after you drive your Alfa into a tree. At the time, I remember feeling pissed at Dave for checking out in such a cowardly way, for not letting his friends and family help him through whatever it was he was dealing with. It seemed like such a rash, impulsive move, and for a while it was hard to really mourn for him when I was so angry at him.

Now, though, I thought about Dave's suicide a little differently. All during my depression I kept closing my eyes and picturing Dave, laid out in his coffin, thinking, *That could be me.* I think I envied him a little, that he had the courage to pull it off, whereas I was all talk. (Oh, man, was I all talk!) Then I'd wonder how strange it was, how unlikely, that three great friends from high school would take turns struggling with depression, each about seven or eight years apart—first Seth, then Dave, and now me. Then I'd think of all the good people out there, dealing with their own depressions, not having the kind of money or support systems or treatment available to them that Seth had had, and that I now had. My depression didn't have to be a death sentence. In this respect, at least, I was one of the lucky ones. Or at least I could be one of the lucky ones, if I didn't screw it up, if I didn't continue along this suicidal course, and yet there I was, all through that spring of 2003, running along one of the main drags in town, thinking, *Phil, all you have to do is lean into the oncoming traffic and your pain will be over.* No, my depression didn't have to be a death sentence. I could hang on until the medications began to work and I could get my life back again, but I seemed determine to check out.

I don't know what it was that held me back, but something did. I'd be jogging, lost in the rhythm of the run, and I'd dart toward the cars, hoping the driver wouldn't have the reflexes to swerve out of my path. At the gym, I thought of letting the weights fall to my chest while I was bench-pressing. I thought of hanging myself in our shed in back of the house. I thought about cutting my wrists. I thought back to tenth-grade science class, when we learned that if you mix ammonia and Clorox together it can create a poisonous gas. I thought of pulling the Alfa into the garage with the top down and closing the garage door behind me, and falling asleep behind the wheel while I let the engine run and the carbon monoxide accumulate and painlessly put me out of my misery. But there was always some miracle to pull me back and keep me breathing, fighting, struggling. . . .

Mar. 17, '03

Still working through these difficult times. I have not felt like me for over a year. I'm trying to move forward but something stops me. I can't figure out why my persona has changed. I've gained a lot of weight. I think I'm emotionally eating. Had to let my suit pants out . . . I'm getting tired of feeling like this empty shell filled with anxiety. Where do I go from here? . . . How long will I be in this holding pattern? . . . Thank God for little Toby. She is life, pure innocence. Keep the faith. Don't stop punching . . .

The Toby aspect was killing me inside. Emme was all broken up about it, too. In some ways, the most distressing part of my illness was that the older Toby got, the more she might someday understand what was happening to her daddy. I'd been depressed—on my way, or deep into it—for most of her little life, but in the beginning Toby couldn't understand that anything was wrong or different about me. Now, however, as she approached her second birthday, she was much more aware of her surroundings and her relationships, and Emme had to help set things up in Toby's head so she was comfortable around me, and around what was happening. The catchphrase Emme used was "Daddy has a boo-boo in his head," which I guess covered a lot of territory. She made sure Toby knew that Daddy's medicines were helping his boo-boo, and that she could never, ever touch those medicines.

The weight gain was interesting. I'd dropped thirty or forty pounds. I had no desire to eat. And then, all of a sudden, I got my appetite back in a big way. There was no explaining it, but that didn't keep my doctors from their theories. They said it might have had to do with a change in my medications. They said it might be a sign that my depression was lifting. Whatever it was, I put the weight back on in just a couple of months. And it wasn't like I was eating healthily or following any kind of regimen. It was mostly ice cream—Häagen-Dazs Vanilla Chocolate Chip and Starbucks Java Chip. Man, I lived for that stuff! For a period of a couple of months, through spring and into early summer, that was my fuel. I'd save the ice-cream binges for the evening, but the thought of them kept me going all day long. I was like an alcoholic, with the thought of that next drink filling my days.

Also during this period, I became a real TV junkie, watching anything and everything, waiting for the sun to set so I could start eating ice cream. That was my world—watching TV and eating ice cream—the whole of my days, for a fairly long stretch. Soap operas, infomercials, old movies, talk shows . . . whatever flicked across the screen. Sometimes I'd have to switch off the TV because I couldn't handle the violence. Even the cartoons struck me as over the top, and the violence would really start to freak me out. My heart rate would just go through the roof. Thank God for the remote control, because I didn't have the energy to get off the couch to change the channel or shut off the set, but at the same time I didn't have the head to keep watching. Some nights, Emme would find me passed out in front of the television set in our den, with an empty pint container of ice cream in my lap or a spoon on my chest, looking like the victim of a hit-and-run at a dairy farm, and she'd coax me into our bedroom and under the covers so I could get a proper night's sleep.

I wasn't getting any better. My doctors thought I was, for a time. Emme thought I was, for a time. Hell, even *I* thought I was getting better for a while there, but I was still in the grip of the depression. I had some good days strewn among the bad days, but for the most part it was one bad day after another, and as I headed into the summer of 2003 Emme had taken full charge of my medications, because I could not always be trusted to follow my doctors' orders.

Here's what I was meant to be taking, on a daily basis:

8 a.m.
  1 Neurontin, 400 mg (one capsule, 2X daily)
  1 aspirin, 325 ml (coated, orange)
  1 Darvon compound, 65 mg (2X daily)

1 Verapimil SR, 240 mg

1 Vitamin B$_1$, 100 mg

1 Xanax, .25–.5 mg

1 multivitamin

4 p.m.

1 Neurontin, 100 mg

1 Darvon compound, 65 mg

1 Vitamin E, 400 unit

1 Xanax, .25–.5 mg

10 p.m.

1 Zyprexa, 7.5 mg

2 Effexor XR, 150 mg

1 Lipitor, 10 mg

And we'd only arrived at this mix, and these dosages, after countless stops and starts and endless trial and error. That's how it goes in a depression. I repeat myself, I know, but it's an important point. Everybody's brain is wired differently, so there's no way to tell how a body is going to respond to a certain set of medications until you try that certain set of medications, and it takes several weeks for some of these medications to take full effect. So the whole process is drawn out, and it can be extremely self-defeating if it takes you especially long to hit on the right combination of drugs; of course, it's even more self-defeating if the patient doesn't follow his doctors' orders and looks to self-medicate from time to time. That's why Emme had to step in and take a more active role in dispensing my medications, because I just couldn't be trusted. I was like a child in this one regard. I used to play with my Ambien dosages in the morning, when

I was trying to wake up, because I found that even though it's a sleep medication it left me with a buzzlike high, a distorted reality, if I took one or two pills first thing in the morning. And believe me, I much preferred the distorted, Ambien-induced reality to the one I was facing on my own.

In mid-July or so, Dr. Wharton shook things up yet again, this time prescribing Zoloft and Depakote, and once again it took my body some time to adjust. Incredibly, I've since read that Zoloft has been proven to cause suicidal tendencies in adolescents under certain circumstances, and yet it remains one of the most common antidepressants on the market. Sometime during my first week on these new meds, Seth came by to tell me our friend Mike had scored us tickets to an Eagles concert in Atlantic City. Seth had spoken to Emme before reaching out to me, and she agreed it would be a good thing for me to get out for some sort of adventure, but I wasn't sure I was up to it. An entire weekend away, down at the Jersey Shore? It seemed like too much, too soon. The Eagles were one of my favorite bands. Seth and I had performed their music together for over twenty-five years. (God, are we *that* old?) Clearly, he and Emme had been thinking the concert might be just the thing to take me out of my head for a few welcome hours, but at just that moment I wanted to stay in bed.

Seth was persistent, and in the end he basically dragged me to the show. He reminded me how things had been for him, and how he also used to feel like curling up in bed and doing nothing. "Where is this getting you, Phil?" he pushed. "You haven't been out of the house for days. But you come with us to Atlantic City, and at least you get to see a great concert."

He had me there, so I dug deep and found the energy to make the trip, and as it turned out it was a great, great show, and a great, great time. Anyway, that's what I was told, because my memory of that weekend is a bit hazy. Why? Well, it turned out too that I was in no shape to be out carousing in Atlantic City in the middle of an unrelenting depression, because in my reckless, irresponsible head I decided it would be okay to have a couple drinks. I don't know what the hell I was thinking. See, when you're taking all those medications, you're supposed to avoid alcohol entirely. That's, like, Depression 101. It's basic. There's no saying for certain how the alcohol interacts with such a potent mix of drugs, but it can't be good, and yet at some point that evening I determined to drink myself into oblivion. I got a little shit-faced. (Well, maybe a *lot* shit-faced!) More than that, I don't remember, although Seth told me later that I seemed mostly fine to him that evening. A little bit more like myself, even, and coming from Seth that's a strong indicator of my behavior. He knew me better than anyone else. If he said I seemed back to my old self, then I must have been back to my old self, and I don't know if that was the alcohol, or the Zoloft and Depakote finally kicking in, or Seth indulging in a little wishful thinking. (Of course, it's also possible that Seth was a little shit-faced himself.) Personally, I don't remember much of anything from that night, but Seth reports that we retreated to Point Pleasant after the concert, and that I took out my guitar and started strumming and singing on the beach, for hours and hours, and that this wonderful group of women happened by and the whole lot of us stayed up all night singing and dancing and having a grand old time. I suppose that's possible. In fact, I'm sure that's how it happened, because I have it on Seth's good authority. But, like I said, I don't have any recollection.

Were there any telltale signs that I would finally attempt to take my life less than a week after that concert? Seth says no. He says it was an uplifting thing, to see me so animated and outgoing after all this time, to hear me singing on the beach, and laughing. The only signs he picked up that night were that I was climbing out of my depression, that the meds appeared to be working, that for these few hours at least I was his brother again.

And then, less than one week later, I very nearly wasn't. It was July 31, 2003, and Emme and I had some sort of fight. I didn't even remember what our argument had been about until I read the account she wrote in the prologue for this book, but what registered was that there was tension between us, and I hated it when there was tension between us. Even when I'm healthy, I don't like it when things aren't right between us, and here, when I was sick, I guess it sent me reeling. I built things up in my head to where I felt I had to do something about it. It's like I was lashing out at Emme, only I wasn't lashing out at Emme—I was seizing on whatever opportunity I could find to put an end to my suffering, and this tension between us seemed to offer just the push I needed.

So what did I do? I climbed the stairs to Toby's room, past the den where Emme was watching television. I was pretty clearheaded, as I recall. And I was crying. The tears had welled up beneath my eyelids in such a way that I couldn't really see straight. Everything seemed blurry. Life seemed blurry. Still, I found my way to Toby's room and stepped inside. There was a night-light on at the far end of the room, but otherwise it was pretty dark. I crossed over to this little mattress where Toby was sleeping—her "big girl" bed, with bumpers along the side to keep her from falling out and rolling around on the floor. Just a couple weeks earlier, I'd had it together enough to disassemble her crib, because she was forever climbing out of the thing and hurtling herself onto the floor, so we figured she'd be safer on the mattress. I knelt down to kiss her. She looked so beautiful, so peaceful. She had this pristine, ivory complexion, like something out of a soap commercial, and I hated what I was about to do to her, to leave her like this.

As I leaned over to kiss her my tears splashed down on her sweet-smelling cheeks. I wiped them dry with the sleeve of my pajamas—a brand-new pair of Hanna Anderssons, green and blue striped, that I haven't had the heart to wear since—but by the time I was through she was wet all over again. I whispered, "I'm sorry, sweetie." And I was— truly, and deeply, and unabashedly. I was sobbing, completely out of it. I knew that this would be the last time I would ever see my daughter, and it was heart-wrenching. I didn't want to wake her, though. I didn't want her to see me crying. I didn't know what I'd say to her. And, more than anything, I didn't want her sweet, innocent voice, or her unfailingly sunny disposition, to pull me back from what I was now determined to do. So I quietly slipped back out of the room and shuffled my way back down the stairs, to the master bathroom, careful to avoid looking in at Emme when I passed by the den, because I knew that if I engaged

Melanie Dunea/CPI

"Familyhood."
Six months
before the down-
hill spiral began.
February 2002.

Stas Rzeznik

"I do." Clinton Inn, Tenafly, New Jersey, November 12, 1989.

"Grandpa" Eric and "Grandma" Bobbie Carle.
Hawley, Massachusetts, September 2001.

"Trick or treat!"
Toby, Emme, and
Emme's sister,
Melanie, host a
neighborhood
Halloween party
at our home.
October 2001.

"Brothers 3"—Seth designed hats for our "brothers only" trip.
St. Maarten, April 2001. (*L to R*) Phil, Jonathan, Seth.

"Ringing in the New Year" January 1968.
(*L to R*) Seth, Jonathan, Phil.

"Phil's fortieth
birthday surprise."
On the ice with
Oksana Baiul.
Fritz Dietl Rink,
Westwood,
New Jersey,
November 2002.

"Birthday boys."
Phil (who had already
lost thirty pounds) and
Seth have never spent a
birthday apart. Grand
opening of the Eric Carle
Museum of Picture Book
Art, Amherst, Massachu-
setts, November 22, 2002.

"Turkey Day."
(*L to R*) Toby,
Melanie, Tonya,
Seth, and Phil
singing together.
Thanksgiving
2002.

"Self-medicating and not looking or feeling great."
St. Barths, February 2003.

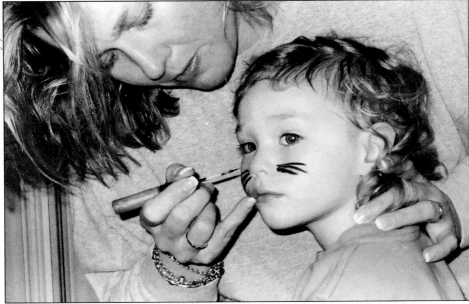

"A few whiskers for our little lion." Emme and Toby on the day
Phil came home from the hospital. Halloween 2003.

"Wanna ride?" Toby and friend "Moosie" on Emme's Vespa—Emme's fortieth birthday gift, which Phil purchased from a pay phone while in the hospital for ECT treatment. November 2003.

"Feeling alive and well." Having fun again!
St. Barths, 2005.

"Family support."
Phil's parents,
Herman and
Judy Aronson.
Cadiar, Spain,
December 2004.

"Loving life!"
It's great to
be able to
laugh again.
Long Beach Island,
New Jersey,
September 2005.

"The possibilities are endless...."
Hotel Christopher, St. Barths, May 2005.

with Emme, the love of my life, I'd lose whatever momentum I had gained.

After I stepped safely past Emme, I stared at myself for the longest time in our bathroom mirror. It's one of those sliding mirrored medicine cabinets, and when I got tired of looking at myself I slid open the door and started pulling out all the old vials of medications I'd been taking for the past year. Most of the stuff in the cabinet was medication that I'd discontinued, for one reason or another, but there were usually several pills left in each vial, and I spilled them all out. For some reason, I took the time to do a mini-inventory in my head, taking note of how many of each medication I was planning to take. I'd empty one vial and then move on to the next. Then I started looking through some of our drawers, and I discovered a few more bottles.

All the while, I kept thinking, *Oh, yeah, I remember taking those.* Or, *I wonder why those didn't work.* Each pill was a trip down memory lane, reminding me of everything I was now determined to forget.

I wasn't thinking anything but to rid myself of the pain and frustration and agony of these past months. I wasn't thinking about which medications made sense to take, or how many pills it made sense to take. I was just grabbing at everything I could find, thinking that all of it, taken together, would be just the right mix. I did this for about five minutes, fisting a handful of pills and swallowing them down—dry—and then fisting another handful. After a while, I wondered if I'd taken enough. I thought, *Should I find another vial?* Or, *Maybe if I take ten of those my heart will slow down to a point where it just won't beat anymore.* I ran through all these different equations and scenarios in my head, trying to hit on just the right mix of meds. Sometimes I'd come across a bottle that was nearly full, and in those cases I only took four or five or six pills and left the rest— although what I was leaving them for, I have no idea.

Some of the pills were coated, and they went down pretty easily. Others nearly choked me, because by the fourth or fifth swallow my mouth was fairly dry, but I got past the gag reflex and finished what I'd started. I took about ten swallows in all, and I was trying to keep track of everything I ingested, but I'm sure I missed a couple meds here and there, and I probably miscounted as well. In all, I probably took nine or ten swallows, and when I figured I'd taken enough I walked to my bedroom and sat down on my side of the bed. I grabbed an envelope that happened to be resting on my nightstand, thinking I should probably write a note. It was just a standard business-size envelope, with the logo and return address of a company in Glenview, Illinois, imprinted on its face. I have no idea what this company does, or makes, or how the envelope came to be lying within easy reach that night, but it did the trick. On it, I listed the medications I'd hastily ingested:

6 Zyprexa
5 Colonopin [*sic*]
8 Xanax
2 Ambien
4 Effexor
5 Zoloft
2 Depakote
2 Verapamill [*sic*]

10 ZYPREXA
5 KLONOPIN
8 XANAX
2 AMBIEN
4 EFFEXOR
6 ZOLOFT
2 DEPAKOTE
2 VERAPAMIN

FUCK ME FOR NOW
FOR NOT BEING AT
FAULT BUT I
INTENDED TO
LISTEN

I'M
SORRY
CAN'T
TAKE
THE
PAIN
ANYMORE
AROUND TO INTERACT
ARE IN REALITY YOU
I'M REALLY SORRY
I LOVE YOU
ALL.

DON'T ANYONE FEEL GUILTY IF YOU'VE DONE THESE THING
GETTING WAY

EMMEG
FORGIVE ME
I'M SORRY THERE SOMEONE AS I KNOW YOU
WILL NEVER BE SOMEONE AS YOU, I KNOW... GOD BLESS ME
AMAZING MALE IT. FOR LOVING SUCH
AND THANK YOU

SETH -
BEYOND THE VIRTUAL YOU TWO
I HAVE I KNOW YOU ARE A PART
AND SEE YOU ARE A PART
OF ME. DON'T GIVE UP
LIKE ME.

JONATHAN MY LIGHT AT RIGHT.
YOU ARE SHIMMERING OF LIGHT.

I ASK AND PRAY THAT GOD WILL
PENSIONE ME.

I recorded thirty-four pills in all, enough to do some serious damage, but I recall taking more. A lot more. I think I even remember realizing that it was stupid to make such a careful note of every medication, so I left off after a while, and figured I could make better use of whatever time I had left scribbling a note.

Here's what I wrote:

Toby, forgive me. I never intended to do this. Listen to Mom and your inner self.

Emme, forgive me. I'm sorry. There will never be someone as amazing as you. I know you will make it. God bless you and thank you for loving me.

Seth, beyond the virtual image I know you find and see you are a part of me. Don't give up like me.

Jonathan, you are my light. Keep shining bright.

General: I'm sorry. Can't take the pain. The ups and downs are to [sic] intense. I'm really sorry. I love you all.

Don't anyone feel guilty. You've been there the entire way.

I ask and pray that God will forgive me.

Next, I shook the watch from my wrist, and set it down on my nightstand. I was tired, and drained. I had been terribly emotional when I went upstairs to say good-bye to Toby, and from there I had become very clinical, deciding which medications to take and which to leave behind, and then when I was writing my note I got very emotional again. I was sad upon sad upon sad, but at the same time I felt this enormous sense of relief. It was a weird kind of peace, and when I was in the middle of it I caught myself looking at my wristwatch for a moment or two. I picked it back up. It had belonged to my grandfather Toby—my daughter's namesake. It was my father's once, and now it was mine. I thought, *Grandpa, you're supposed to be watching over me, and you're not doing such a good job of it.* He'd always been one of my favorite people, and I let my mind run to what he might make of all this, of looking down and seeing me trying to take my own life. Then, on an impulse, I threw the watch to the floor and started stomping on it with my heel. Smashed the crystal face into a million pieces. I'm not entirely sure why I did this, but I guess I was so completely and totally pissed with myself and everyone else on the planet that crushing my grandfather's watch must have struck me as some kind of end. It was symbolic. I didn't think it through; I just did it, and in the doing there was a strange kind of release.

Then I lay back down on my pillow and tried to sleep.

I look at that watch now, more than two years later, and I wonder if I'll ever get around to fixing it. I suppose I should. It's a beautiful timepiece, and a treasured family heirloom. But it sits in my bureau, its face smashed to bits, its mechanism probably all shot to hell, and it's as if time has stood still, since that dark, despairing night. And I look at that note as well, and I wonder at my uncertain handwriting, and I try to put myself back in the frame of mind that drove me to try to take my own life in the first place, but those impulses are lost to me. Thank God. I didn't realize it at the time, but it was such a transparent cry for help—a cliché!—especially with the way I listed all those medications, like I wanted to make it easy for the paramedics and EMT guys I knew would find me, so that they might undo what I was so feebly attempting.

I Can't Believe He Didn't Say Good-Bye

EMME

We all knew something like this might happen. That's where we'd been headed for over a year, with all of Phil's talk about killing himself—all of it becoming more vivid and more specific as time dragged on. So it's not like it took us completely by surprise, him taking all those pills, but at the same time it was a shock to walk into the bedroom one morning and find my husband semiconscious, his eyes rolling around in his head, a suicide note by the side of his bed and all these empty vials lying around in the bathroom.

It's like someone pulled the rug out from under me.

The irony here is that we'd been talking about an institution, someplace where Phil could be monitored and treated and kept from his own impulses until he could get past his depression, but every time it came up his doctors would ultimately say his condition wasn't serious enough.

I'd hear that and think, *He's talking about driving his car into a tree! Hello! What is your idea of serious?* And yet underneath that type of thinking was a kind of denial, because I guess I didn't want to admit that I had a husband who needed to be institutionalized. I might have pushed harder to have Phil committed, but I guess I wasn't ready to face that that's where we'd fallen.

Clearly, Phil was in a full-blown, all-encompassing clinical depression, and we all should have known something like this was without question a reality. It was inevitable, and you don't have to be a doctor to know that if you're on a collision course the thing to do is change course. (Duh!) I don't mean to lay blame, because Phil's doctors were wonderful, and they truly did have Phil's best interests at heart, as did I, but I stated earlier that there were times when we might have been a little more proactive, and this was most definitely one of those times. We should never have let Phil's condition deteriorate to where he could carry out an attempt on his own life—and yet when we were in the middle of it I guess we all felt we had a handle on things, that we could get from one day to the next and string a bunch of weeks together, and give the meds a chance to do their thing and the illness a chance to run its course without taking any drastic measures.

The lesson here, for readers going through these same circumstances, is that some of these so-called *drastic* treatment measures aren't really all that drastic. Here's what I mean: I'd heard from friends about a couple in Massachusetts, with one spouse who had been battling depression for more than thirty years, and the deal they made with each other and with their doctor was that any time the husband began to go south, any time he began to experience symptoms of his recurring depression and start to feel things were careening out of control, the wife would drive him to this hospital they had picked out near their home and check him in. It was all prearranged. And it's not like she was abandoning him or anything, not by any stretch. She'd visit him every day, and he'd get the treatment he needed, and he would be in a nurturing, protective environment until his moods leveled off and his meds began to kick in, and there wouldn't be all this disruption to their household, or their family, and there wouldn't be this constant uncertainty, and this waiting-for-the-other-shoe-to-drop nightmare that we had experienced for the previous year and a half. They didn't think of it as an institution, or having the husband committed, or any of those negative buzzwords that too often attach themselves to our clear thinking on mental health issues. Not at all. To this Massachusetts couple, it was just the logical next step, after all else had failed.

Let me tell you, that *so* would have been the move for us, if I could have just gotten together with our doctors to make it happen in time to prevent something like this, because in our case all else was clearly failing, but nobody seemed to think Phil was an appropriate candidate. Even Phil didn't see himself as a candidate! Still, I looked high and low for a place where I could keep Phil safe, an institution or a program that was set up to deal with his self-destructive impulses. I scoured the Internet. I talked to friends, and friends of friends . . . anyone who had some personal experience in this area, and it's amazing how many people I found who

had some information to share, once I went looking. Ultimately, my search led us nowhere, primarily because Phil
wouldn't get on board. For all his talk and obsession with
killing himself, he didn't get that this was where he was
headed, that this was what he so desperately needed, and
right or wrong I couldn't bring myself to move aggressively
on this front without Phil's involvement.

Back to the nightmare scene unfolding in our bedroom,
and the blow that nearly wiped us out. Liora, my sister-in-
law, was over in a flash, and so were the EMT guys, and the
local police. The swift response was just incredible, although even those few minutes seemed like hours after I set
the phone back down and turned my attention back to Phil.
Liora whisked Toby away to another part of the house, so
she wouldn't have to experience the scene, and at some
point in the middle of all this commotion and emotion I remember looking at this envelope Phil had left behind on his
night table and shaking my head at the way he listed all the
medications he'd taken. I was crying, and frantic with
worry, but I can laugh about it now—a little bit—at how
anal he was, how compulsive, even when he was trying to
kill himself. I thought, *That's my husband.* Really, it was Phil
in a nutshell—meticulous and organized to what he must
have thought was the very end.

Everything happened so fast. Phil was in and out of con-
sciousness as they checked him out in the bedroom. His eyes
were all over the place. It was almost eerie. They'd be closed,
and then they'd flash open and seem to furiously scan the
scene, and then they'd close again, and all the while it wasn't
clear to any of us that anything was registering for him. He

wasn't really lucid. He mumbled and groaned, but I don't think he was in any pain, and I don't think he said anything. He told me later that as he was being wheeled out to the ambulance he caught sight of our neighbor, who had come out to his front yard to see what all the commotion was, and that he had this look of great concern on his face. *I* didn't even notice that, and Phil barely seemed to notice me, but this is what registered. And it checked out, too. Our neighbor was indeed outside, and he was of course concerned, and somehow his presence filtered through, so Phil was at least somewhat aware of his surroundings.

I rode in the ambulance with Phil, and I'd like to write that I held his hand and stroked his forehead and kept whispering that I loved him the entire way, but I was consigned to the front seat, and the only help I could be was to tell the driver to go faster—which I guess meant that I was no help at all. Anyway, I don't know that I had the head for that kind of loving attentiveness at just that moment. I do know that Phil was so out of it he couldn't talk, and that he seemed to keep nodding in and out, but I don't know if I had the strength or the intestinal fortitude to say anything to him. Really, my head was all over the place. I was sad, and angry, and frantic, and confused—and, of course, relieved that there was a good chance Phil would make it through this okay. Things were looking up, and I tried to find the silver lining in that. At some point, this sense of relief became my prevailing emotion, and I started to look at this suicide attempt as a symptom of Phil's illness and not as something over which he had any control.

You know, the line you hear about suicide attempts among patients in a depression is that it's a cry for help, and in some cases it's probably a cliché, but in Phil's case I think that's really what it was. He didn't want to die, it's clear to me now. He wanted to kill the pain of the depression. He didn't want to check out and never see me or Toby or his family ever again. He wanted to escape. He didn't want to miss out on the stories of our lives before we could finish writing them. He wanted to let us know that he needed some help with this thing. That's all it was to him, how he processed it, and in time I came to understand this. At just that moment, however, I struggled to make sense out of it. As soon as Phil was stable, and his vital signs were checking out okay, I began to feel like this was a real turning-point moment for us and that things could only get better. And yet underneath that relief was a welling anger. I kept thinking, *He didn't say good-bye to me. That son of a bitch, I can't believe he didn't say good-bye.* I looked on as they were working on him, and I kept coming back to this one thought, and to be honest it took several months of sessions with my therapist to work all the way through it, but I came to realize that it wasn't Phil. It was the depression. Whatever anger I had initially, that he could be so selfish, to try to take his life, to leave me and Toby without a father and husband, to leave without saying good-bye . . . got put into perspective as the reality of the depression set in. (Thank God for therapy.)

The deal with the police and the EMT unit was that they had to take Phil to the closest hospital. That's how it goes in most jurisdictions, but all of our doctors were affiliated with

Columbia Presbyterian in Manhattan, so I tried to buck procedure and have Phil taken there, but in the end they had to rush him to the emergency room at Englewood Hospital. When we finally got to the hospital, and they strapped Phil into this bed on the emergency unit, and started hooking up all these intravenous tubes and monitors, that's the first I remember actually sitting with Phil and holding his hand and stroking his hair. That's when those loving and attentive genes kicked in. I kissed him on the forehead, and told him I loved him, and that everything was going to be okay. And it wasn't just a line—I believed it! Fully and wholeheartedly. Then I stepped out into the waiting room to check in with our family, and as soon as I saw my mother-in-law and my sister-in-law I burst into tears. I'd been holding it in all that time, since we'd left the house, and the floodgates just opened. I said, "I can't believe he actually tried to kill himself! He's so sick. He's just so sick. Can't anybody see what's happening here?"

Of course, this was just me venting, and overstating the obvious, but I was emotionally spent, frustrated, and concerned. Plus, I'd become conditioned to thinking that we were swimming upstream with this thing, going against everybody else's current, to where my default approach was to push hard for every piece of attention I could get from Phil's ever-widening circle of caregivers. *Can't anybody see what's happening here?* Everybody could see what was happening, but I guess I was programmed to think I was the only one. I had never gone through this before, although I would later learn this was the bottom line when mental health professionals deal with the spouse of a patient in a depression, to keep that patient safe. *Just keep Phil safe,* that was the mantra, but I kept hearing it as everybody seeming just a little too calm for such a drastic situation.

I had all this anger bubbling over inside, so much that it even spilled into the waiting room, when I should have simply been relieved that Phil was going to be okay. I was a complete mess, and it's a good thing I was swallowed up by the loving embrace of my mother-in-law and my sister-in-law and everyone else who eventually turned up—including my brother, Chip, who cut short a business trip to be at my side—or else I might have just clawed through the plastic cushions on the waiting room chairs. (Thank God for family, too.)

Amazingly, I still had to conduct business for Emme Associates, because no one at work outside of Amy knew what was going on with Phil. I even had to give a telephone interview to promote our Emme Collection, and I hated that I had to give a telephone interview, but there was nothing I could do for Phil at that point, and I guess I thought it would be a good distraction. Let me tell you, it was one of the weirdest, most incongruous moments of this whole ordeal, to have to duck outside of the emergency room to make a cell phone call to some reporter, and to pretend to talk enthusiastically about our new clothing line, while inside the hospital my husband was recovering from a suicide attempt. I'm sure it was a terrible interview, but for some reason at just that moment I thought the thing to do was press on. Eventually I did confide to a trusted colleague at the Collection that Phil was in the hospital, and she was enormously helpful in postponing my appointments for the next few days, but I was bouncing back and forth between doing what was right for our business and doing what was right for me and Phil, and not having any clear idea on either end. I guess I got caught up in the same impulse that found my in-laws all those years earlier, with Seth's depression. I didn't want such a deeply personal matter to seep its way into the workplace, because I worried it might have some negative impact on our business relationships going forward. It's pretty amazing—don't you think?—that no matter how en-lightened we *think* we are, we're still trudging through the Dark Ages on some of these things.

Englewood Hospital is our local hospital, and it happens to be a great facility. They've even got a psychiatric ward, and it's relatively quiet, but we all felt Phil needed to be where his team of doctors could take proper care of him, where they all had privileges, and I spent most of the rest of that day has-sling with our insurance company and with various hospital administrators, trying to jump all the hurdles we needed to clear in order to get Phil transferred to Columbia. Dr. Whar-ton, too, was a giant help in effecting Phil's eventual move to Columbia, but even with his inside track it was no easy feat to bring about the move. Still, the complicated transfer was a place to put my bundled-up energy, something to focus on other than the fact that my husband had just tried to kill him-self. Anyway, that's where we needed to be; that's where he could get the cutting-edge treatment he desperately needed.

In fact, the real "cutting-edge" treatment wasn't really cutting edge at all—it had been around for generations, and it was still so controversial that Phil resisted it the first time it was presented to him as an option in his case. It didn't really come up until he was on the psych unit at Columbia, but I'll mention it here because it was all-important: electroconvulsive therapy, or ECT. Phil's doctors weren't all that convinced that the therapy would be called for in Phil's case, but it was the next treatment we had to consider, especially since we were over a year and a half into this thing and the medications still hadn't gotten the depression under control, and he was now on a full-fledged suicide watch. Nothing else seemed to be working.

As soon as the doctors laid it out for him, Phil was spooked by the ECT procedure, from all those old movies where they'd give patients a violent series of electrical shocks to the brain. His initial response was to wave it off, and I can't say I blamed him. The thinking in lay circles is that ECT is *only* for people suffering from severe mental illness, or that it's something out of *One Flew Over the Cuckoo's Nest* or *A Beautiful Mind,* but the truth is that it's commonly used in treating patients like Phil, patients suffering from mood disorders like depression or acute mania, or certain types of schizophrenia. Suicidal patients like Phil who can't wait for their antidepressant medications to take effect have also had good success with ECT.

Here's how it works: Doctors administer an electrical stimulus meant to induce a general seizure, which in turn kick-starts the brain in such a way that it begins to set things right. At least, that's the idea. None of the doctors I spoke to could pinpoint exactly why the therapy works, or precisely what the seizure does to the brain, and the literature isn't all that clear on it, but it does work, in many, many cases—sort of like a restart button on your computer. Back in the 1940s and 1950s, when it was known in some circles as electro*shock* treatment, ECT was seen as a last-resort therapy; the patient's entire body would convulse with the seizure, and as a result it came across as an extremely violent, aggressive, perhaps even barbaric form of treatment. At least, that's how it always registered for me—and apparently for Phil as well. But these days the patient is given general anesthesia and a muscle relaxant that is meant to cover all parts of the body except one or two extremities, like a finger. Wherever the muscle relaxant doesn't reach, that's where the body experiences the seizure, so there's none of that violent, all-over shaking that you used to see. Plus, the present "shock" is now administered as a carefully monitored electric stimulation therapy (EST). It's all quite civilized and benign and painless, and after a couple minutes the patient awakens with no memory of the treatment itself. The procedure is repeated every third day or so, usually running from six to twelve treatments, or more if needed. Under certain circumstances, treatment is suspended if other, unrelated conditions persist or appear to put the patient at risk. In Phil's case, for example, his atrial fibrillation sometimes caused his heart to race, to the point that his cardiologist would be unable to sign off on a scheduled treatment until his heart rate returned to normal levels. That situation always put us on edge, because it threatened to prolong his stay on the unit, which in turn put our insurance in jeopardy.

While he was walking us through the origins of ECT, Dr. Wharton shared an interesting side note, which suggests that this type of treatment is as old as recorded history. He told us that shocks from certain "electric" fish were known to have recuperative effects on some fishermen, according to ancient Greek and Egyptian history. As a result, these fish—electric eels in the Aegean, and electric catfish in the Nile—were held out as an important staple in a healthful diet.

Okay, so that was our little history lesson on ECT. The continuing controversy over the treatment, we learned, has less to do with its seemingly brutal beginnings in our mental institutions than with its present-day side effects, which can range from headaches to persistent (and, in some cases, permanent) memory loss and posttreatment confusion. Also, experts are split on whether or not the treatment is indeed effective. Some studies show as much as 80 percent improvement in patients suffering from severe depression, while others show such a high rate of relapse that some doctors regard it as a wash. And yet even with all this controversy, more than a hundred thousand patients submit to the therapy each year, after reaching the point in their treatment where nothing else has seemed to work. That's where we were, right after Phil's suicide attempt, but we weren't ready to sign on for the ECT just yet, so we signed on instead for a heavy-duty course of new meds and hoped for the best.

Whether or not we ended up going the ECT route, we wanted to be on the psychiatric unit at Columbia. We wanted to be with doctors who knew Phil and his recent history. At Englewood, he was just being seen by the attending physicians in the emergency room, and then after a day or so they transferred him to the psychiatric unit there.

The psych unit at Englewood was in desperate need of a makeover. It was painted in a pale, surgical green, which struck me as one of the most depressing colors they could have chosen. (Really, who comes up with pale surgical green?) Phil was assigned to a double room, but there was no roommate, which I took as a blessing. He was in no shape for a roommate. I'd duck out for a moment, to see about the insurance hassle, or to talk to one of the doctors, and come back to find Phil curled in a fetal position, rocking to some silent rhythm. Sometimes he'd be mumbling, "I don't want to be here, I don't want to be here, I don't want to be here," and I'd have to fight back the impulse to join him—because, believe me, I did not want to be there either.

Anyway, Phil's condition was quickly stabilized, and I turned my attention to completing paperwork and pulling strings and hassling with the insurance company to arrange for his transfer to Columbia Presbyterian. I had to jump through all these ridiculous hoops, and when it became clear that the insurance wouldn't cover his entire stay at Columbia, I arranged for it anyway. I figured I could fight about the money later. We weren't *Beverly Hillbillies* rich, not by any stretch, but we had enough money in the bank to cover what I thought at the time would just be a couple nights in the hospital. All I cared about at just that moment was getting Phil set up with the best possible care, in the best possible facility. Nothing against the good people at Englewood Hospital, but Columbia was the place I felt he needed to be.

Phil had a ton of visitors at Columbia Presbyterian. He ended up making three extended visits there—the first, immediately following his suicide attempt, when we hoped that a new course of medications might be the answer; the second, when it was apparent even to Phil that the meds were just not working and we needed to sign on for the ECT; and the third, when the first course of seven ECT treatments appeared insufficient and we had to go back for three more. (So much for thinking it would be just a couple nights in the hospital!) We're really blessed with a strong, supportive network of family and friends, and they turned up during each of Phil's extended stays to offer whatever help they could. Even Jonathan made the supreme effort to come to the hospital to visit his big brother—on his birthday, no less—and with his trademark good cheer, he couldn't resist giving Phil a little dig. He said, "Yeah, this is really where I wanted to spend my birthday." He was in a wheelchair by this point, and it was difficult for him to get around, and my mother-in-law had to do pretty much everything for him, but he wanted to be there for Phil. That's how it was with most everyone in our circle; they wanted to be there for Phil, and it was so nourishing to be surrounded by so much love at such a stressful time.

Before Phil could even get settled on the unit, we met with Dr. Milica Stefanovic to discuss the ECT. Phil's parents, Judy and Herman, and his brother Seth joined us, because we believed it was important to include the whole family. (Jonathan would make it to Nine Garden North, the psych unit at Columbia Presbyterian, for a couple visits, but he wasn't feeling up to this family powwow, otherwise he would have been there as well.) Dr. Stefanovic detailed all the benefits, and all the possible side effects, and helped us to weigh the pros and cons. She was extremely patient with us, and pretty honest about the controversy surrounding that type of treatment, but she stressed that they'd had a good success rate with it. We all had some serious concerns, and we took turns voicing them. One of my biggest concerns was the pain associated with the treatment. After all, they administer a general anesthetic, so I naturally assumed it was a painful procedure, but Dr. Stefanovic assured me that there would be no pain and that the only reason they put the patient under was to control some of the involuntary muscle responses and to reduce anxiety.

As it played out, ECT wasn't the only way to go. Along with Dr. Wharton, Dr. Stefanovic also gave us another option, which was to try some new cocktail of drugs. They had just started Phil on new meds about two weeks prior to his suicide attempt, so clearly that mix wasn't right for him.

We were all a little scared of the ECT, despite Dr. Stefanovic's mostly positive description. Phil was frightened to death of it, and he was very much in favor of trying some new mix of medications, and ultimately that's what we did. And so for two weeks during his first stay on Nine Garden North, we gave the drugs one last shot, with the understanding that if we didn't see some marked improvement in Phil's moods and levels we would revisit the idea of ECT.

Very quickly, we established our new routines—which of course we had to build around the hospital's routines. Visiting hours were in the afternoon and evening, and I made sure there was always someone to keep Phil company, to occupy his mind and distract him from the monotony of his days. You were only allowed two visitors at a time, so I had to keep everyone on a kind of schedule.

Sometimes, when he had visitors, Phil would take out his guitar and play a couple songs. Sometimes they'd watch television. Sometimes they'd play Scrabble, although Seth reports that Phil seemed to have a faraway look in his eyes. He'd manage to put words on the board, which I guess was a good indicator of his ability to concentrate on a simple game like Scrabble, but from time to time you'd look over and see him lost in some bizarre little rhythmic motion, like making a half karate chop with one hand against the wrist of the other, over and over and over. It was a mannerism we'd never seen out of Phil before, and we didn't know what to make of it, but there it was.

I'd try to do every lunchtime visit, and I made a big deal out of bringing Phil something exciting to eat each day. He wasn't crazy about the food on the unit, so I brought in pizza and sushi and great sandwiches. I tried to mix it up, and keep it interesting, and when his friends came by during the evening visiting hours I'd usually ask one of them to bring up dinner. It was really sweet of them to do it, and I thought it meant everything to Phil, to have something really good to eat, so by the end of his stay he was probably the best-fed patient in the history of Nine Garden North. If I could have found a way to send up breakfast for him, I would have done that too. He didn't always have the best appetite, mind you, but I thought it was important that he take an interest in food, and that there be some variety in his diet.

In the evenings, I'd be at home with Toby, trying to give her some semblance of a normal home life. In a lot of ways, I was like a single parent all through Phil's illness, but at this time especially. I had an enormous amount of help, but at the end of the day it was just the two of us, mother and daughter, trying to find our footing. As I wrote earlier, Toby truly was an easy toddler. She never cried, and hardly ever fussed, but even the easiest toddler in the world can be a handful. It's a wearying thing to have to take care of a small child all by yourself, especially when you're doing so on top of another wearying thing like taking care of your husband who just tried to kill himself.

I was only able to bring Toby to Nine Garden North two or three times during Phil's entire stay, and those visits were always poignant for the way she could peel past the setting and still find her daddy. Anyway, she'd go looking for him. She'd say, "Daddy, I want you to come home. Why can't you come home?" And it just about broke my heart. One time, she took Phil by the hand just outside the double security doors located at the entrance to the unit, saying, "Time to go home now, Daddy. Your boo-boo's all better." It was hard, because she wasn't allowed all the way onto the unit, so we had to do our visiting in this tiny space by the security doors, and it was also hard because their time together was so short.

Whenever Toby and I were home, and the house was quiet, our conversations always turned around to Phil. He was in our thoughts, and in our prayers. We actually got into the habit of saying prayers each night, beginning when Phil first started to not feel well, and we continued the habit all through his hospitalization. (Happily, we continue it to this day!) We'd pray for him to get better, and to come back home. Toby would also sneak in these perfectly age-appropriate appeals, thanking God for the tulips and the butterflies and the rainbows, and then she'd turn to me and say, "Daddy likes that." It was so sweet. She had just turned two, so she was very much aware that something was different in our household. She could pick up on my tension and sadness, and all she had to do was hold her arms out for a hug, and for a moment I'd forget the baseline uncertainties that had become a constant in our lives.

Sometimes Toby would make Phil a cute little picture, and I'd bring it to the hospital the next day and he would look at it and just cry and cry. I'd look at him, and I'd start to lose it, too. It got to where I couldn't bring him *all* of Toby's little pictures, because it was just too painful to watch him break down like that—for both of us.

As I recall, Toby slept in my bed a whole lot during the time Phil was in the hospital, and I'm sure it was as much for her as it was for me. It couldn't have been easy for her to understand and process what was happening. (Hell, it wasn't easy for any of us adults, so how in the world could it have been easy for a two-year-old?) When she started nursery school, just a few weeks after Phil was admitted onto Nine Garden North, she had some real separation issues. This was the first piece of parenting difficulty I encountered, and I realized she might have had these issues anyway, even if her daddy wasn't on the psychiatric unit of a New York City hospital, but we had to work through them just the same. There were some days when I would have to sit in Toby's classroom for two or three hours, reading a newspaper or a magazine, watching the clock because I knew I needed to get into Manhattan in time for Phil's visiting hours, and those classroom hours seemed endless. I wanted to be with Phil, and I needed to be with Phil, but at the same time I wanted and needed to be with Toby. I was the very definition of torn. I had it set up with Toby's teacher that she would give me a signal when she thought it was okay for me to leave, and I remember feeling like I couldn't be there fully for my daughter or for my husband.

For his second stretch at Columbia, we had to arrange it so that Phil would be admitted on an emergency basis, which meant he'd have to spend at least one night in the psychiatric emergency room, and even then it wasn't a done deal. Even then there was no guarantee there'd be a bed for him on Nine Garden North, despite Dr. Wharton's extra efforts to arrange for one. As a matter of fact, when we got to Columbia for this second tour, I had to leave Phil on his own while I went to the billing office to make all the arrangements, and it took such an impossibly long time. I had to slog through this unexpected insurance nonsense, and sign all these commitment papers. For some reason, the insurance company had no record of Phil in their computer, even though he'd already been there just a few weeks earlier, and it was the most frustrating thing to have to deal with something as mundane as paperwork and insurance in the middle of everything else we were going through.

Meanwhile, Phil had been ushered into the psych ER, and by the time I got to him, maybe an hour or so later, there was only a short time left on the posted visiting hours; I had learned from Phil's first stay that the folks at Columbia Presbyterian were serious about their visiting hours, so I knew we only had a few minutes before I'd have to go home that first night. I took a good look around, because I wanted to get my bearings and to truly understand what Phil might be facing—and what he was facing was a nightmare beyond anything we'd experienced so far. Like the Nine Garden North psych unit upstairs, the psych ER at Columbia Presbyterian was separated from the waiting room area by two steel doors, with small glass windows that allow you to see through to either side. Unlike Nine Garden North, however, the place is crowded, and claustrophobic, and teeming with all kinds of dangerously psychotic patients, detoxing patients, and patients in various need of restraining or sedating. It was a real horror show— and poor Phil was right in the middle of it!

The deal is you announce who you are, and who you're going to visit, and you get buzzed past the first door, so that you're momentarily inside this small vestibule-type area between the two doors, and then when the first door shuts you get buzzed past the second door and onto the ER floor. Really, they don't mess around with security. That was the first thing I noticed about the place, and it kind of set me on edge right off the bat. The next thing I noticed, after I'd been buzzed in, was a whole wall of noise, like an unrelenting ruckus of sound and confusion, and I wondered how these hard-to-handle patients could ever hope to heal in the middle of such a racket. I looked out among the chaos and saw four or five gurneys set off in this walled-off area, behind Plexiglas, lined up in a kind of holding pattern. Next to one gurney there was a guy pacing back and forth, and back and forth, like a caged tiger. His body was covered with tattoos. He wore a hospital gown, so there was a lot of skin showing, and all of it was tattooed—head to toe, and front to back—and the guy made a real menacing appearance. His eyes were dilated, and he just kept pacing, and mumbling, and looking like he was fixing to pounce. On what, I had no idea, and I didn't particularly want to stick around to find out.

On one of the other gurneys, there was a middle-aged man being restrained by two attendants, so that they could inject some type of medication into his veins to calm him down. The poor man seemed to be hallucinating, and lolling his head from side to side, and resisting the efforts of the two attendants.

Next to another gurney there was an older African-American man, spewing out the worst racial slurs I could imagine—about women, and Asians, and Puerto Ricans—and I couldn't remember the last time I'd heard such a colorful diatribe. The weird thing about this guy was that he had no teeth, and his eyes seemed to be empty, like there was nothing going on behind them, and the words just kept coming out of his mouth without emotion, like he'd committed his ranting to memory, or was reading off a list.

Strangely, once I was let in to this walled-off Plexiglas area, my first thought was for my own safety. Isn't it funny, the way the mind works in times of great stress and uncertainty, the odd things you focus on? There were armed guards and nurses and attendants all around, but I looked down at this mesh top I happened to be wearing, with a layering piece underneath, and for a beat or two I thought, *Oh, dear God, I'm going into the pit. These people are just going to tear me to pieces.* Really, I thought I was going to be killed. When I left the house that morning, the outfit didn't seem revealing or provocative in any way, but here, in this context, amidst all this madness, it seemed completely inappropriate, and I managed a slight nod in the direction of the crazed tattooed tiger, I guess maybe to see if I could tame him with kindness.

People ask me all the time what it was like to move about the hospital and muscle through our ordeal beneath the strange light of celebrity, and these weird fleeting thoughts about my inappropriate top offer an appropriate point of reflection. Yes, I'd lived a pretty glamorous life, for the previous ten or so years. My working days had been filled with fashion shoots, and movie premieres, and public appearances, and I always relished being the center of attention. You don't go into a career like modeling if you don't like being in the spotlight—and baby, I *loved* being in the spotlight. But even before Phil's depression, I wanted to tone down the sometimes harsh glare of celebrity when I first got pregnant with Toby. After she was born, I pulled back on the public part of my schedule, and obviously I had to set aside any modeling gigs until I could once again look my best. Once Phil got sick, however, the modeling and the celebrity and the glamour were the furthest things from my mind. Some mornings I'd catch myself looking in my closet for something to wear and wonder if I'd ever again reach for some of the more provocative outfits I had hanging in there. I thought maybe that part of my life was finished.

There was one particularly weird celebrity moment, back before Phil was hospitalized, that left me thinking I lived and worked on such a strange plain. I was asked to be a guest host of Montel Williams' syndicated talk show, and to interview Montel about his own depression, and at some point in that studio, talking to my friend about his harrowing personal ordeal, my mind naturally wandered to Phil and the depression that was threatening our own lives at home. I thought, *Gee, Emme, things are just so bizarre.*

Did I disappear from the public eye because I was ashamed of Phil's depression? Absolutely not. I did check out, for a time, but only because my focus was elsewhere, and it took moments like this one, walking onto the emergency psych unit with my "revealing" top, to get me to realize how startlingly different my days had become. So that was the scene, and it was fairly overwhelming, and I quickly scanned the room looking for Phil and found him curled up in that fetal position again, on one of the other gurneys, facing the wall like he was trying to tune out the ruckus and commotion all around, like he wanted to be any place else in the whole world. I took one look at him and thought, *Oh my God, that's my husband.* It was heartbreaking to see him like that, to know that this was where he belonged, among all these wild, sick people, that this was really what was best for him. I tried to picture him healthy and whole, but all I could see at just that moment was this wounded shell of a human being. I wondered at how far we'd fallen, since those first signs of chronic pain almost two years earlier. And I wondered if we would fall farther still. It was the kind of situation I'd never thought we'd find ourselves in, and yet here we were, thick in the middle of it, and hoping for the best.

"Hi, sweetheart," I said to Phil as I sidled up to him from behind, in the most soothing voice I could muster.

"I'm here." I collected him in a sidelong hug. "We're here now," I said. "Everything's going to be okay."

"This is pretty crazy, isn't it?" Phil said, still facing the wall, away from me, and sounding surprisingly like his old self.

"Yep," I said. "Pretty crazy."

And it was, but at the same time it felt exactly right. *Pretty crazy and exactly right*—the story of our life these past months. All that commotion aside, I told myself that this psych ward was exactly where we needed to be, and that the ECT would be exactly what we needed—to set things right for Phil, to take us back to how things were—and as I pulled back from that moment I realized what a strange picture we must have made. The hardly glamorous super-model, holding on for dear life to her hardly lucid super-husband, set against the horrific backdrop of the psychiatric ward of a New York City hospital.

I went home that night, with Phil still curled up on that gurney, still facing away from the commotion, still willing himself to some other place, and it tore me up inside to have to leave him like that, but they were pretty strict about their visiting hours. I went home to my Phil-less house, and when I stepped inside it was like the whole energy of the house had changed. I'd seen traces of that change during Phil's first extended stay at Columbia, and here it was again. Toby was sleeping in her room upstairs, and after I sent the babysitter home I went in to check on her, and I remember being over-come by this uplifting sense of peace. She looked so sweet, so innocent, so completely and blissfully unaware of the tur-moil that had swallowed up her family, and I let myself get caught up in that bliss. Usually, when Phil was off on one of his getaways with his brothers, I'd pine after him and there'd be a really empty feeling around the house, but on this night it wasn't like that at all. On this night, there was just this cascading relief that seemed to wash over me, and I kept thinking, *Okay, we're out of it now, the worst is behind us.* And do you know what? That night, I had the best sleep I'd had in months and months. Actually, it was the best sleep I'd had in years, because in the beginning I was breast-feeding Toby, so I was up all the time for that, and then as Phil's depression dragged on I was up constantly and sleeping fitfully because he was always roaming around the house at night, and rummaging through the bathroom, and it always felt like I had to keep tabs on him. But here, at long last, I fell into a deep, restful sleep.

All this time, on the other side of the Hudson, Dr. Wharton was working his magic, helping us to cut through all that hospital red tape, and he managed to snag Phil a room on Nine Garden North, and by the next morning Phil was moved from the holding area on the psych ER unit, away from all that noise and craziness, and onto the main psych ward. The bed came through just about the time our insurance was finally approved, so at least we had that hassle behind us—for the time being, anyway.

Nine Garden North

PHIL

I guess one way to tell how many friends you have is to try to kill yourself and see how many people turn up—either at your funeral, or at the hospital where you'll inevitably be taken if you fall short of your goal.

I don't mean to come off as glib (which as most of us who follow this sort of thing know by now is what Tom Cruise called NBC's Matt Lauer during one of his rants against antidepressants), because as I look back through the fog of those dark days immediately following my suicide attempt, I'm struck by the outpouring of love and support from friends and family. God, it was amazing—and all-important. Who knew there were so many people who gave a shit about me? Who knew my life intersected with so many others? Who knew people could be so giving, so caring, so concerned? They came out of the woodwork: people

I hadn't seen in years, people I knew only to nod hello to in town, people from work who wanted to share their own experiences with depression. They'd call, or write letters or e-mails, or check with Emme to see if I was up for a visit. (Truth be told, more often than not I wasn't, but Emme knew how important it was to keep me connected to the outside world, so she told them to come by anyway.)

Even the people from my group therapy sessions came up to the unit to see me, which I thought was absolutely incredible. I mean, I'd only been to group a couple times, over a stretch of a couple weeks, and I didn't think I'd made any kind of real connection to these folks. Dr. Sonty thought it was important for me to give group a shot, but it didn't do anything for me. Nothing against any of the other patients, but as I wrote earlier, I didn't have the head to listen to other people's stories, and I didn't have the energy to share mine. Yet here they were, as a group, trekking up to the psych unit at Columbia Presbyterian; they'd come in two at a time because of the tight visiting regulations in place, while the rest of them waited for me just on the other side of the double security doors, all of them wanting to let me know they were pulling for me and that we were all on this ship together. We hadn't connected on any kind of personal level, but the fact that we were going through the same struggles, and teetering on the same brink, put us on a kind of common ground—and it was enough to draw them near.

It seems like a small thing now in the retelling, but at the time it was everything. I drew enormous strength from these visits. Really and truly. It was better than any cocktail of antidepressants, better than any jolt I could have gotten from the electroconvulsive therapy everybody seemed to want me to take. Like I said, if it was up to me, I'd have told these good people to stay away, but Emme knew better. She knew I needed to be surrounded by love and good cheer and support—to be swallowed up by it, if such a thing was possible. The folks from group, they were able to shore me up and set me straight and remind me that I was not alone. They didn't even have to say anything; their presence alone told me that I wasn't the first person to suffer through a depression, and that I wouldn't be the last. No, sir. And it wasn't just the folks from group who picked me up. Soon enough, there were new friends on the unit at Nine Garden North, patients like me who had been riding the terrifying roller coaster of depression, many of whom were undergoing their own ECT treatments and sharing their experiences with me. There were friends from around town. People I knew from work. My parents, who wanted to come every day. Even my brother Jonathan made it to the hospital, sick as he was, and it was such an ordeal for him to move about, but he made the extra effort. Each call or note or visit was like a lifeline, and I clung to it.

Aug. 14, '03

I'm hanging in. This morning was tough. I hope I've bottomed out and I really am trying to make each day count. The new meds don't seem any different. Nothing's really changed. Nothing much matters to me at times. I'm up and down like a yo-yo! I feel that I'm in this race that does not want to end. I know I have to remain positive but there is a part of me that just wants to give up. I can truly appreciate and understand when someone is not well. I know I will pull through this. I have to. Emme's trying so hard to keep me on track. So is Seth, Mom, Dad and Jonathan, too. He's my hero! I can't believe his spirit. People react to things in their own way and unfortunately I'm not doing as well as I'd hoped to be.

My three extended stays at Columbia seem to run into one another in memory. I was so out of it during most of that time it's amazing to me that I remember anything at all, but there are snippets and snapshots that pop out as I look back. I remember that there was a pay phone out in the main living area of Nine Garden North, and that's where we made and received calls. It was a real center of activity on the unit, because of course cell phones weren't allowed. My friend Jacci gave me a phone card so it would be easy for me to reach out to other people, and I thought that was about the nicest, most thoughtful gesture; most days I put it to good use, but I would always have to wait my turn for the phone. There was only the one pay phone, and it was almost always in use. In some ways, it made the place feel like a college dorm. You'd get a call, and someone would come looking for you. Or you'd be on the line and someone would be slumped along the wall nearby, waiting impatiently for you to finish. For a lot of patients on the unit, especially those who didn't have such a strong network of friends and family available to visit, the phone was a focal point of their time on Nine Garden North—their one real link to the outside world.

My first room faced the George Washington Bridge—the kind of wonderful view tourists would pay top dollar for at one of Manhattan's better hotels, and from what I've since learned about our health insurance and the amount of money we had to pay out of pocket to cover some of the hospital costs, I guess you could say we paid top dollar for it, too. Talk about a paradox! That bridge had been a real focal point of my depression, in a negative way, and now it loomed as a focus of my hospitalization—hopefully, in a positive way. I spent most of my first few days on the unit sleeping, or pretending to sleep to avoid interacting with the staff and the other patients. For all the buttressing and support I might have gotten just from the sheer number of people around me, I wasn't in the market for new friends at just that moment. I didn't want to hear from anyone else on the unit. When I wasn't in bed, I was looking out the window at my wonderful view. That was my one real link to the outside world. I'd take in the endless stream of cars driving back and forth to and from the city and wonder if I'd ever be able to drive across the bridge again. I kept thinking, *Will I ever return to "normal" and commute into the city like I'd done my entire adult life?* Or, *Who do I talk to in order to get my old life back to where I can sit in all that bridge traffic without being a threat to myself or to anyone else?* I don't know if the administrators who designed the Nine Garden North unit had this view in mind when they laid out the facility, but the bridge and everything it represented was a constant and powerful reminder to me of the life I left behind, and to which I longed to return.

The routine was that we'd line up first thing each morning to have our temperatures taken. Then they'd take our blood pressure, sitting and standing, and after that we were weighed. It was a real assembly-line operation, most mornings. Also, they kept checking our bags, and our personal belongings. The staff would constantly go through our stuff, to make sure we weren't hoarding any type of object that could do harm to ourselves or to others. I suppose they had to do this to keep us safe, from ourselves and I suppose in some instances from each other, and if you had visitors they'd do a search every time your guests left the unit; whenever they did, I used to think, *Yeah, someone's going to give their depressed friend a jackknife. Just the gift for the buddy who tried to take his own life just a few days earlier.*

There was this one guy on staff named Barnes who usually did the honors each morning, getting us up and out of bed and started with our day. He was the perfect man for the job, like someone sent from Central Casting. I liked him a lot. In many ways, Barnes became the soul of Nine Garden North for me. He was a big, strong, bald African-American, and a real gentle giant—for some reason, I found his presence on the unit to be a great comfort. And yet despite Barnes's cheerful disposition, I wanted nothing to do with him in the morning. All I wanted was to sleep. In this one respect, at least, my time at Nine Garden North wasn't that much different from my time at home, and I wanted to pass most of it with my head against a pillow. Plus, I hated waiting on those lines to have my temperature and blood pressure taken, so I usually stayed in bed until Barnes made his second or third trip past my room. I guess I was so used to Emme and Toby coming in to sing me awake with their special good-morning song that I needed more than one wake-up call to get going. I needed a whole *routine*.

If I wanted to shave, I'd have to go see Barnes or someone else on the staff, and he'd go back into a locker area where they kept our cosmetics bags and shaving kits. Then he'd follow me to the bathroom and hand me my razor and stand right behind me while I shaved, so the whole time I could see my face in the mirror and his face looking right back at me, from over my shoulder. I always thought that was weird, and a little unsettling, the way Barnes's big, bald head kept hovering in the background. When I was finished, I'd hand the razor back to Barnes and he would return it to my shaving kit and lock it back up.

There was another attendant named Milton, another good guy. When I'd been on the unit a couple weeks, I started noodling around with an idea for a children's book, and I actually wound up writing and rough-sketching the whole thing during my stay. I'm really proud of how it turned out, and I'm looking forward to finding the right publisher for it, but at the time it was just something to do, a place to put my creative energy. I ended up calling the main character Milton the Multitasker. That's the kind of impression this guy made on me. Poor Milton the Multitasker took on so many responsibilities that he couldn't keep up with them, and I look back and think he was mirroring all the responsibilities I'd taken on in my own life: managing Emme's career, becoming a father, and on and on. I had a couple of creative outbursts like that at Nine

Garden North. I also wrote a song on my guitar—"Show Me the Way"—with a lyric that still touches my heart every time I sing it, and takes me back to my mind-set in those dark, uncertain weeks:

Hard times ahead, been there before
Seems like the darkness keeps knocking at my door

Keep up the faith, don't let your guard down
It's never easy when evil comes around

Buildings are falling, scattered lives abound
Reach out with love and turn insane around

CHORUS:
What can I do? What shall I do?
You've got to let go, let God take him by the hand
He'll show you the way to be
Let go, let God take him by the hand
He'll show you the way to be free

Muster the courage, strength and trust
It's been so long now, I'm starting to rust

Can't control the feelings, intense pain inside
Take off your seat belt, let's go for a ride

I'm scrambled in my head, lying in my bed
A mouth full of pills and I could be dead

CHORUS:
What can I do? What shall I do?
You've got to let go, let God take him by the hand
He'll show you the way to be
Let go, let God take him by the hand
He'll show you the way to be free

Show me the way . . .
Please, show me the way . . .

At some point, early on in my stay, Emme had brought my guitar up to the unit, and it was such a welcome gift. Especially now that I wasn't doing all that well, I longed for the guitar, so that I could lose myself once again in the lilting rhythms of the thing. It's like it held some magic power. For the first couple days I just played quietly in my room, but after a while I played for all the patients and the attendants, and everyone seemed to look forward to it. It turned into a real sing-along . . . the only thing missing was the campfire. This happened a couple times, as I recall. Some nights, I wouldn't feel up to it, but then someone would come by and tell me how everyone was looking forward to the music and the singing and the camaraderie, so I'd suck it up and play. (It's like the song says, you have to give the people what they want, right?)

A word or two on my guitar, that all-important lifeline: you know, it's funny, but with all that security, and all these extra precautions they would take to protect us from ourselves, no one ever bothered to check my guitar case. I could have had a machine gun in there, for all these guards knew. In addition to my extra set of strings, a tuning fork, and picks, I also kept a pair of pliers to clip the excess strings in case I had to do some restringing, and if you were hell-bent on self-destruction you could do some serious damage with a pair of needle-nose pliers with a sharp edge.

Anyway, after we weighed in, we'd get breakfast. The food wasn't lousy, but it wasn't particularly good, either, and Emme saw to it that I had some wonderful things to eat during afternoon and evening visiting hours, from any of several outside restaurants. For breakfast, though, I was on my own. On the unit, they dispensed our food from metal carts, almost like the ones flight attendants wheel down the aisle on the plane. In every slot, there'd be a tray with someone's breakfast, whatever you ordered from the night before, or whatever your doctor or nutritionist had instructed you to eat, depending on your situation. The staff would call out our names, and we would get up and take our trays back to the tables and eat. Sometimes I'd eat alone, and sometimes I'd sit with some of the other patients. We'd get our meds in our rooms, or on the fly; the nurses or attendants would track us down and hand us a little cup and wait while we swallowed it all down. Half the time, I had no idea what I was taking. All I remember specifically was a little plum-colored pill—Seroquel, which was noticeable for the way its color stood out. I used to spot it in my cup of medications and think, *Hey, there's that little plum-colored guy.* It was like a little psych-unit game I played with myself, finding the plum-colored pill in the sea of reds and whites and blues and creams, like finding the NINAs in those Al Hirschfeld drawings in the Sunday *Times*.

I was a bit of a loner my first few days on the unit, although I did make a couple friends early on, and once I got comfortable there I made friends more easily. I met this one girl, Christa, when I was checking myself into the psych ER for my second hospitalization, while Emme was dealing with all of our insurance crap. We were sitting in the waiting room, me and this other girl, and we flashed each other these *holy shit!*–type looks—you know, like *I want to get out of here, too.* And right there we formed one of those neat, right place–right time connections. It turned out Christa was going through some serious bipolar stuff, and when we got up onto the unit we compared notes a little bit. That's how most of these connections started. You'd catch yourself eavesdropping on somebody else's craziness, and you'd look up and see someone else eavesdropping on the same deal, and you'd lock eyes and form a quick little bond, like there was now some great secret between you.

That's how I met most of my friends on Nine Garden North, with this knowing eye contact, with an innate understanding of the deep shit we were all in together. And we came from all walks of life into that deep shit. We were a regular melting pot: rappers and lawyers; people on welfare and people of extreme wealth; people of all different races, and ages, and intellectual backgrounds . . . all of us in every shape, size and stripe of mental illness and depression. There was even a New York City police officer on the unit, a good guy who'd been down at the World Trade Center on September 11, struggling with post-traumatic stress disorder, and growing a bushy beard that seemed to want to reach to the floor.

Still, I kept mostly to myself for the first couple days. I don't think I had any visitors just yet, other than Emme and Seth and my parents, but if I wasn't out in the living area with them I was back in my room, trying to sleep, or looking out the window at the George Washington Bridge, or quietly strumming my guitar. My friend Israel brought me a CD player with earphones, and I listened to a lot of music: Seals & Croft, Loggins & Messina, America, Simon & Garfunkel, Billy Joel, Jim Croce, Dan Fogelberg . . . all of my old favorites. I'd heard these songs so many times the music was almost a part of me, and I was happy to lose myself in it again and again and again. It helped to make these new surroundings a little bit more familiar, to put a soundtrack I recognized beneath a scene I could not.

I slept a lot. And I dreamed a lot, too. I'd dream of being chased. I'd dream of being better. I'd dream of the ocean and cool breezes. I'd dream of being younger. This last was a little unusual, even for me, because when I was well I rarely dreamed of me as anything other than my present age. I had this one recurring dream when I was with Jonathan, and he was strong and happy. I'd had versions of this same dream before I was on the psych unit, and I've had them since, but they all run pretty much the same. We're by a lake, somewhere in the country, and Jonathan's pushing a wheelchair, and at some point there's this strange reveal and I notice that the strong and happy Jonathan, with his full head of hair, is pushing the sick and frail Jonathan. The sick Jonathan is usually hunched over and looking like crap, while the healthy Jonathan is always strong and handsome and completely in charge. And then the healthy Jonathan turns to me and says, "Don't worry, it's going to be all right." I had that dream a bunch of times while I was on the unit, and I never knew quite what to make of it. I didn't know if that was Jonathan telling me things would be okay, or if that was me telling Jonathan to hang in there just a little bit longer, or what, and before I could figure it out there'd be Barnes hollering at me in his deep, powerful voice to get a move on.

For the first couple weeks, my doctors were experimenting with an aggressive new mix of antidepressants. That was the plan, to give the medications one more try before considering the electroconvulsive therapy. Initially I was terrified of ECT, and determined for the drugs to work. As soon as I got on the unit, however, the doctors sat us down and walked us through the ECT treatments, and still all I could think about was Jack Nicholson in *One Flew Over the Cuckoo's Nest*. Remember how zapped and out of it he appeared when he came back from those treatments? I couldn't get past the "shock therapy" aspects of it, even though Dr. Wharton and Dr. Stefanovic kept insisting that the "shock" had really been taken out of the procedure. It was all very safe and civilized, they said. They even told me about a cutting-edge technology called electromagnetic therapy, which kept the seizures to an absolute minimum, but I wasn't prepared to give myself over to any of this stuff just yet.

I remember talking a lot to a friend of mine whose father had been through six depressions, and had undergone three or four ECT treatments, and he really swore by it. He said, "Phil, you've really got to consider this." He said it was like magic, but I wasn't looking for magic. I had a hard enough time dwelling in reality. I couldn't really trust my memory, because I couldn't concentrate enough to read, or to identify the people in old family photos, so I had to trust Emme and my family to do whatever research they could manage and report back to me with any interesting information, but my gut told me to steer clear. I remember asking Dr. Stefanovic if the treatment was always successful, and she told me it wasn't. I asked if people ever died from it, and she told me that on rare occasions that could happen; statistically, it happens once every ten thousand cases—that's roughly ten times per year in the United States alone—and it's usually owing to human error of some kind or other: either the equipment isn't used properly, or the current is directed toward the precisely *wrong* spot, or the patient doesn't turn out to be such a great candidate for the treatment after all.

Everyone was holding out all this great hope for the ECT, and not much hope for the new meds, but I didn't want to be a statistic, and I didn't want to be like Nicholson's Randle Patrick McMurphy character in *Cuckoo's Nest*, so we all agreed to give the new meds a chance. While we were waiting, it fell to me to make the most of my time on the "psycho" unit, as I came to call it. There were about two dozen other patients on the unit at any given time. It was actually pretty civilized—a real healing environment. There was a very nice dayroom area, with a television and lots of bookshelves. There was a computer station, where you were allowed to sign up for Internet access. Maggie, from the recreational staff, would let you log on for fifteen minutes at a time, and I remember I was working so slowly that it felt like less than a minute. I thought maybe I'd check my e-mail, but I only got through one or two messages before my time was up. There was an exercise room with some bare-bones equipment in it. They even had a trainer-type person show up a couple days a week, and she put me on a reasonable-enough routine that I tried to do each day, but it was mostly hit or miss. Some days I felt up to it, some days I didn't, even though I knew it was important for someone like me, because I needed to keep physically active to raise my serotonin levels. There was also an arts and crafts room, with beads and clay and markers and whatever we might need to divert our attentions from the drudgery of our days, but I rarely took advantage of it. I was always retreating to my room—to sleep, or listen to music, or just be by myself and stare out across the Hudson—and one of the staff would always be coming in trying to coax me out, to get me to participate in group, to interact with the other patients on the unit, to take part in some activity or other. Emme remembers that the nurses and attendants had to pretty much beg me to come out of my room and take part in the goings-on around the unit, but in the beginning I wasn't getting off my bed if I didn't absolutely have to.

I was a tough "nut" to crack—get it?—but after some persistence I would usually come out and participate in some of the activities happening around the unit. Once, in a kind of group therapy workshop, I was handed a sheet of paper with the heading "I Will Like Myself from A–Z." On it, I was supposed to come up with twenty-six adjectives to describe myself, from A to Z, and the idea was that my responses would be in some way revealing.

Here's what I wrote:

A. Awesome/Amazing

B. Buff

C. Creative

D. Decent

E. Energizing

F. Family man

G. Generous

H. Happy

I. Intelligent

J. Joker

K. Kind

L. Lover

M. Mindful

N. Neat

O. Outrageous

P. Pleasing

Q. Quiet

R. Righteous

S. Sensitive

T. Trustworthy

U. Unbelievable

V. Vain

W. Wild

X. "Exceptional"

Y. Youthful

Z. Zany

It's telling, I think, that I saw myself as "Positive Phil," and yet I didn't feel positive, and even then I wondered at the space between my idealized image and my reality. (It's telling, too, that right off the bat I couldn't decide between "awesome" or "amazing," which I guess is a good indication of how full of shit I can be when I'm idealizing myself.) Hell, if you'd asked anyone of my acquaintance, they could never have guessed that I was describing myself in this list. Probably the only word that accurately described my persona at the time was "quiet"—and that's only because there aren't a whole lot of *q* words I could have put down instead. *(Quixotic? Quick-witted? Quizzical?)* At one time, sure, I was the positive guy I described in my alphabet, but I hadn't been that guy in over two years, and I worried if I would ever be that guy again. It was an old snapshot, and that was one of the most difficult aspects of my depression, knowing what I was capable of and still not being able to pull it off. The best way I can think to describe this feeling is to compare it to someone who might have lost his hearing or his eyesight. Can you imagine what that must be like? To know that you were once able to listen to music, or the sound of a waterfall, and to no longer be able to hear anything? Man, that must be tough. To have seen the sunset, and the mountains, and the ocean, and yourself in the mirror, and to have to now live in a world of darkness? To look into the eyes of your soul mate and then never see them again? That's got to be just awful, don't you think?

But that was me. That was how the depression changed my perspective. I was someone who once gushed positive energy and happiness and enthusiasm, and now all I gave off were these killing, negative vibes, and that's what I was struggling with. Every day, every waking moment . . . this was my struggle. The thing about going through something like this on a psychiatric unit at a major metropolitan hospital is that you're constantly reminded that the struggle is not yours alone. This can be a great, reassuring thing, if you're open to it—only I wasn't always open to it. It can also be depressing in its own right, to look on at these faces of despair and hopelessness and realize that this was where you belonged, this was what you had become.

I know I wrote earlier that I clung to all my personal connections and friendships like a lifeline, but there were also times when I was at Nine Garden North when I chose to keep to myself. There was group therapy available to us on a daily basis, sometimes two or three times a day, but I didn't go to too many of these sessions. I preferred to talk things through with Dr. Wharton or Dr. Stefanovic one on one, when they came by on their rounds. With Dr. Wharton, it wasn't like one of our private sessions back in his office, but some days we'd sit and talk for a half hour or so, and that's where I found my comfort and reassurance. For some reason, I decided that I would be available on the unit to help others, in whatever ways I could manage, but that I didn't need any help from anybody else. I would go it alone—also, completely *not* like me, but this became my mind-set from time to time.

Very quickly, I realized that the meds weren't about to make a difference—at least not on the timetable I very much wanted—and the more I hung around these other patients going through their ECT treatments, the more I saw how it seemed to roll off of them like nothing at all, the less weirded out I started to be about the procedure. During my second stay at the hospital, for example, my roommate was a supernice young man named Sateesh, and he was undergoing the first of his ECT treatments when I arrived on the unit; I could actually see a change in his demeanor after my first few weeks there. I also noticed that he was never anxious about each approaching treatment. He seemed to look at it like no big deal, like he was off to get an injection or an X-ray, so watching him go through it really eased some of my concerns. Sateesh was about fifteen years younger than I, but we had a lot in common. He also listened to his CD player all day long, so we talked about music. And we talked about our struggle with depression. I was thrilled for Sateesh that he appeared to be getting better, but I felt bad for him. He was a cutter; he had these major scars running along his wrists, forearms and chest, and I could never understand how someone would cut into their skin with razor blades to try to kill themselves. It seemed so unnecessarily painful. Of course, who the hell was I to talk, right? I mean, I'd just swallowed ten fistfuls of pills to try to kill myself, so I wasn't exactly qualified to pass judgment on someone else's behavior in this department. Self-mutilation? That was Sateesh's thing, not mine.

Ultimately, about three weeks into my first stay at Columbia Presbyterian, the clock on my insurance coverage began to tick more and more loudly. That was always the big question, in the back of our minds and underneath almost every conversation we had about my care: how much would our insurance cover, and for how long? After three or four weeks, it was clear that the new meds hadn't brought about any kind of miracle cure, but at the same time I was relatively stable and no longer perceived to be a threat to myself, so they sent me home. I was thrilled to get back to my own bed and my old routines, but at the same time a part of me knew I wasn't ready. And it turned out I wasn't. I was still deeply depressed, still moving about in a constant haze, still unable to connect with other people in any kind of meaningful way . . . and after another week or so at home I decided to give the ECT a try. Just like that. I figured, hey, I'm not getting any better on the medication, and I'm not really able to function at home on my own, so I might as well see what else Dr. Wharton and company have in their bag of tricks.

Whatever had me spooked about the ECT when it was first laid out as an option now struck me as nothing at all. I guess the proximity to it while I was on the unit and my growing familiarity with it just wore me down, and the new meds just weren't working. I was anxious for results. Very quickly, I'd gotten to the point where I would have tried anything, so Emme set off on this wild odyssey with our insurance company, while Dr. Wharton and Dr. Stefanovic made arrangements to have me readmitted. As Emme described, this was when they had to check me in through the psychiatric emergency room, because that was the only way they could swing it with our insurance company.

My doctors prescribed a series of seven treatments to start. They didn't know if that would be enough to "zap" me back to my old self, but figured that would be a good jumping-off point. If needed, they could always prescribe additional treatments later, Dr. Wharton said. He also told me that, more and more, people were referring to it as electric stimulation therapy, which I guess sounds so much more benign. I mean, from a marketing perspective, if I was going to take a treatment like this and make it more appealing to a potential user, I'd move people away from thinking about convulsions and seizures and shock treatment. Makes sense, doesn't it? *Stimulation* seemed to give the treatment a much more positive spin. Anyway, I didn't get more comfortable with it until I was able to think in terms of its therapeutic benefits, and when I finally did I was open to it.

One of the doctors compared the jolt of electrical current that would briefly run through my system to what it would take to run a hundred-watt lightbulb, so on my first trip to the ECT lab I joked to the anesthesiologist that I should put a lightbulb in my mouth during the procedure, like Uncle Fester from *The Addams Family.* "Hey," I said, "at the very least I'd have a brighter outlook on this whole nightmare."

Well, *I* thought it was funny.

Once I decided to go ahead with the ECT treatments, I allowed hope back into my life. This was a curious and welcome thing, because it had been months and months since I let myself look ahead, at what the rest of my life might bring. Everything had been put on hold, for all this time. I was still not well, and I still had a long way to go, but I began to have a strong feeling that this was the path I needed to take. Where there was once doubt and fear there was now hope and confidence. I knew I couldn't go any lower than I was the night I tried to take my life. I had already crashed. There was no place to go but up.

Dr. Wharton was right—the treatment itself was no big deal, no different than going under to have one of your teeth pulled or a cavity filled, something most of us don't even think twice about. I didn't really remember a whole lot about it once I was through. It took just a couple minutes, and I was out cold the entire time, and when I was through Emme was waiting for me in the recovery room. They wheeled me out in a wheelchair that first time, and Emme said I looked a little dazed and addled immediately afterward, and that my hair was messed and smushy from all the gel they had to put on my head in order to help activate the electrodes, but we just sat quietly for a while, holding hands. After a few minutes, Emme asked how I was doing, and I didn't respond. (I have no recollection of that first session—or of any of the sessions, really—but this is what Emme tells me.) One thing I do know is that I never experienced any pain, and it was never weird or uncomfortable or disconcerting. There were always a couple doctors and attendants in the ECT lab with me, and once or twice they had to postpone the procedure because my heart rate wasn't exactly right—owing to my afib, I guess. They really took every precaution. And, of course, I had to wait those couple days between treatments, because it takes a lot out of you, getting zapped like that, and you can't just run through those seven treatments back-to-back-to-back. You have to give the brain time to respond.

The doctor who conducted the ECT treatments was always immaculately dressed. It's like Emme said, it's funny the things you notice at times like these, but this is what registered. She wore matching suits: jacket, skirt, the whole deal. I don't think she repeated the same outfit once during the run of my treatments, and I remember thinking how monotonous her job must have been, and that maybe that was why she spent so much time on her look, just to spice up her days a little bit. Sure, she was helping people, and providing a valuable service, and all those good things, but I couldn't get past the drudgery. Think about it: she snaps the electrodes on your head, or behind your ear; she puts the goop on your head; she switches on the machine. And that's it. Over and over. All day, every day. She was very professional, but it struck me as a boring job—she was a doctor, after all, and each time out I caught myself hoping she did more than just these ECT procedures.

Very quickly, I found myself looking forward to these treatments for that brief moment before the anesthesia would kick in. Before I'd go under, the doctor would tell me to count backward from one hundred, or something distracting like that, and I'd always try to fight it, to prolong that moment, because it was inside that moment that everything else fell away: the depression, the pain, the uncertainty. . . . It was the one pocket of time I had to be completely and totally unaware of anything that was going on, and after everything I'd been through it was such pure bliss that I never wanted it to end.

Once I started with the ECT treatments, I fell into a kind of routine. My visitors came more frequently, although I had some trouble remembering who had visited and what we had done or talked about. That was one of the bad side effects of the ECT, the way it played with my short-term memory. I recall watching a lot of television in the dayroom on the unit, but I could never remember what I had just watched. I played Scrabble. I played the guitar. I worked on my children's book. I looked forward to my next visit, or treatment, or session with one of my doctors, because I told myself that with each visit, or treatment, or session I was inching ever closer to the day I could go home. That was always the carrot at the end of the stick for me, going home, but then I'd look up at the end of the day and have trouble remembering what I'd done all afternoon.

I don't know that I was really up for all those visitors, because folks are still telling me how out of it I was when they came by, or they want to know what was up with this strange little karate chop mannerism I'd developed, where I'd lapse into this staccato-like rhythm, chopping gently against my opposite wrist. (Actually, one of the therapists I visited suggested this chopping motion as a distraction, and I guess it became a habit.) They'll tell me about something that happened when they were visiting me in the hospital, and I'll have no idea what they're talking about. Sometimes they'd report back to Emme that I was pretty lethargic, or not making much sense, and Emme would ask me about it the next day and I wouldn't even remember that they'd been by. It scared the crap out of me, all this stuff going on right under my nose with me having no recollection of it, but Dr. Wharton and Dr. Stefanovic were able to assure us that this was probably just a side effect of the ECT and nothing to worry about.

Sometimes I was completely "there" for a visit, and those moments of course stand out. I remember Toby's visits, naturally, because they were a real highlight. It broke my heart to have her see me like that, but I was wearing my own clothes, and I dug deep to find whatever pieces of "Positive Phil" were lurking at the subsurfaces of my brain. She wouldn't even notice any of the odd behavior all around, or the sterile surroundings; she'd just run into my arms and hold tight in the biggest, juiciest, warmest hugs I could have ever imagined, and I'd try not to cry. Emme's since told me that she tried to rehearse Toby a little bit before these visits, to warn her what to expect, but that Toby wasn't much interested in being rehearsed. She'd say, "Daddy's boo-boo is getting better," and that was all that mattered to her.

I also remember one night when Seth was by, and so was our friend Jacci, and we were hanging out, and playing guitar, and talking. The plan was for Seth's wife, Liora, to come up and join Seth at some point, only when she did they wouldn't let her on the unit because I was allowed just two visitors at a time. The security guard who controlled the door during visiting hours was a real hard-ass named Rufus. At least that's how I thought of him back then. He was just doing his job, I realize now, but it always felt like he was busting our chops.

We tried to sneak Liora past Rufus by telling her to sign in as a guest of one of the other patients who didn't have any visitors that evening, but Rufus wasn't buying it. Finally, he came over to us and said, "If you want your friend to come onto the unit, one of you is going to have to leave."

I said, "Okay, I'll go!"

Once again, *I* thought it was funny. So did Seth and Jacci, but they were a friendly audience. Rufus was a much tougher room, and if he had any sense of humor he certainly didn't show it, although we got along well enough after this one "confrontation." Anyway, the line put me in mind of the old switcheroos Seth and I used to pull as kids. After all, we were identical twins. This was our wheelhouse. Who would ever know if I switched clothes with Seth and walked out the door? It would have been just like the character of Chief in *Cuckoo's Nest*, only I wouldn't have to throw a sink through one of the hospital windows to bust loose. I'd just look smart and snappy in Seth's suit, wave good-bye, and stroll out of there without a care in the world. So I turned to Seth and said, "Want to stand in for me?" And we talked about it, and laughed about it, and kicked it around for a while; we even ran through a couple scenarios to see how things might go. And—who knows?—Seth might have gone for the idea for an evening, and there's no doubt in my mind that we could have pulled it off, but I was scheduled for another ECT treatment the following morning.

I had a hard time focusing—another side effect of the ECT. I couldn't read. I could make out signs, or short sentences, but show me a full paragraph or a page of text in a book and I'd stare at it for the longest time and still have no idea what it said. I also had a tough time expressing myself. My vocabulary was very limited. I'd find myself in conversations where my mind would be thinking one thing while my mouth was saying something completely different. I'd do my new karate chop move on my left arm whenever I was searching for a word. It was the most frustrating thing, not to be able to articulate what I was feeling, thinking, seeing. . . .

After about four or five ECT treatments, I began to notice

a positive difference, beyond these few negative side effects. And it was just like Dr. Wharton and Dr. Stefanovic had predicted: the good seemed to outweigh the bad. I became a little more assertive, a little more productive, a little more energetic. It was hardly a seismic shift, and it's possible no one else noticed but me and perhaps Emme, but each day I seemed to discover a piece of the old me I hadn't seen for the past two years, and every new piece seemed to go looking for another, and at one point I realized I'd moved a long way back to whole. At least, that's how it felt to me, and I suppose it's possible it was just another case of wishful thinking, but I wanted so desperately to believe in it. You have to realize, there were only a couple ECT treatments left on Dr. Wharton and Dr. Stefanovic's initial prescription, and our insurance company was telling Emme that our days at Columbia Presbyterian were numbered, and all around me patients were getting discharged and returning to their old lives, and all this stuff must have conspired in my racing imagination to get me thinking about going home. And soon.

Back and Forth
(and Back and Forth)

EMME

I think we jumped the gun a little bit, that's how anxious we were to reach the happy ending to Phil's story—and, as you'll see, how anxious I still am after finally reaching it.

In any case, following Phil's first five or six ECT treatments, we started convincing Dr. Wharton and the other professionals involved in Phil's care that Phil was getting better, that the shock therapy was working. And it was, too, so it didn't take much convincing. (Our insurance company, meanwhile, was quite adamant about it: they cut off our coverage after just seven treatments, concluding that they were all Phil needed to get back up to speed.) Coming out of each treatment, Phil would be pretty much out of it for the rest of the day, but by the next afternoon he was much more focused than he'd been, much more engaged and "in the moment."

It's like each treatment shook off another layer of the depression, like we were peeling away at an onion and the real Phil lay in wait inside, and I think the onion metaphor is appropriate because I couldn't help but tear up as I watched what was happening. I *knew* this was what my husband needed, I *knew* he was getting better, and I *knew* there was no alternative, but it tore me up inside to have to watch it. Goodness, I wouldn't wish this kind of ordeal on anybody—on either end, Phil's or mine—because it was grueling, brutal, heartbreaking. A couple of times, I went home at night and caught myself crying, because it can really rattle you to see the person you love put through these harrowing paces, to see him have to endure these shock treatments, to know what it's doing to his body.

Look, as much as I resisted it at first, and as much as it might still make me a little uncomfortable, I'm a big proponent of ECT; in Phil's case it turned out to be a lifesaver, but no matter how they dress it up and make it seem less intimidating, there's no mistaking it for anything else. It is what it is, and it's pretty much terrifying to close your eyes and picture what happens to your husband in the ECT room, so I tried to put my mind on something else whenever he went in, and I was thrilled when Dr. Wharton told us Phil could go home after his seventh treatment. I'd had just about enough.

Dr. Stefanovic suggested we consider another few treatments, just to be on the safe side, but she also thought it would be okay to suspend the treatments and go home, if that's what we wanted. I didn't think *I* could take much more of it, so this was a welcome development.

Of course, Phil didn't go home right away. It's not like

they wheeled him out after that seventh treatment and pronounced him cured and fit and good to go. That would be the sappy, Hollywood ending, but that's not at all how it happened. There was a stretch of days in there when we had to figure some things out, and during that stretch I began to doubt that he was ready to go home after all. Phil had a couple of "sessions" with Dr. Wharton and some of the other doctors monitoring his case. There was talk about how to manage our insurance crisis, which was a constant theme of Phil's hospitalization, but also how it was probably prudent to suspend the ECT too soon rather than overdo it. The thinking was that Phil could always go back for another few treatments if it was determined that's what he needed—almost like a tune-up is how the doctors described it. Remember, each treatment could potentially shave off whole chunks of memory, and there was an understanding that you didn't want to undertake more treatments than were absolutely necessary.

All of a sudden, Phil seemed to get a whole lot better. He really did. More and more, he was alert, and focused, and positive. More and more, he seemed to get back those pieces of memory that were momentarily lost to the ECT. More and more, he seemed like an active participant in his own life, instead of the coolly detached observer he had been for the past months. There was a clarity about him that had been missing for the longest time. And yet at the same time, more and more, I caught myself second-guessing the doctors, and doubting all these positive signs. Was he really ready to go home? I wondered. Would I really be able to look after him? Would we ever get our lives back and return to how things were before the chronic pain?

Still, I felt an enormous sense of relief once Phil's depression "lifted"—although on this first pass it didn't exactly lift all the way away. Yes, it was like things were about to pop right back into place, right where we'd left them all those months ago, almost like we could will it so. And yes, we were probably getting ahead of ourselves a bit, but I think the two of us were so anxious to get on with our lives that we seized on every hopeful development as some kind of signal that the worst was behind us. And it was, it's just that we still had a ways to go.

Phil's doctors kept reminding me about the memory loss, and that some of Phil's memories might be gone for good. Certainly, some of the things that happened on the unit, during the run of his ECT treatments, he might never piece back together, but we were hoping that the rest of the picture would fill itself in. I must confess, I was a little terrified that the man I was bringing home would be somewhat different from the man I married, that maybe the piece that reminded him why he loved me in the first place might have fallen away. There was this weird pressure between us to get back to how we were, as quickly as possible. Anyway, *I* felt it. It's possible I was even responsible for it. I can't say for sure what Phil was feeling at the time, but I think we were both pushing things along a little bit, force-feeding ourselves the idea that he was well and back to his old self, even though he wasn't quite there.

Even before the ECT, we went home from that first stay in the hospital willing Phil back to normal. He wasn't there yet, but that's where we all needed him to be. I'll backtrack a bit and explain. We'd tried that aggressive new course of meds during Phil's first stay on Nine Garden North, and when the doctors finally sent him home I was torn. I'd been looking forward to his coming home for the longest time, but when the moment was upon us, I realized he wasn't ready. He still seemed so far gone to me at times. Better, but far gone. Not all there. And, like I said, when he was being discharged from the psych unit, after the new meds had had about a month to kick in, I didn't trust it. I was *so* ready for this ordeal to be over, but looking back it's clear that Phil *so* wasn't ready to come home. Almost as soon as he got back into our bedroom, some of those old patterns began to emerge. The fatigue. The inability to get up off the bed. The staring off into space. The not making sense. The inability to string together a complete sentence. The disinterest in friends and family. There had been all this great progress, of a kind, and now he seemed to take a step back for every step he had taken forward. Toby was the only thing that brought a smile to Phil's face, and she would bound into our room without a care in the world and Phil would just light up like the Phil of old, and I would think, *We're so close!* It was all so *right there,* and yet at the same time it seemed further out of reach than ever before. That was the most frustrating part of those first few days, with Phil just home from the hospital the first time, how close we had been to getting the old Phil back, and with each day at home it seemed we were inching away from it.

I don't think I handled things too well, with Phil home from the hospital. I don't think I was ready to be disappointed, to fall from the hopeful highs we had felt when we left Nine Garden North to the worrisome lows of this next phase, so we stole away to the beach for a couple days with Toby, just to escape the tension that had suddenly crept back into our home. I thought perhaps that a change of scenery would put us all on our best behavior. You have to realize, when Phil was up at Columbia Presbyterian, Toby and I had developed this nice routine, and our house had become a kind of safe, peaceful haven, but when Phil was back home and still struggling there was a black cloud about the place, the way there'd been for all those months before he tried to take his life.

At times, Phil had great difficulty making himself understood. It's like he knew what he wanted to say but couldn't get it out, and he fell into this habit of hitting himself in the leg repeatedly until he either came up with the word or phrase he was reaching for or he came up blank. (This behavior was more pronounced after his second set of ECT treatments, but there were elements in place even before his first round.) He wasn't ready to drive; he couldn't even navigate his way around town. Even shopping for food at the supermarket was a frustration. I'd leave him alone for a minute and come back to find him standing stock-still in one of the aisles, overwhelmed by all the products and packages on the shelves, like there were just too many options to consider and his brain had shut down against the overload.

And yet all of these setbacks would have been manageable if it wasn't for the uncertainty that came along with them. The not knowing if the depression was behind us. Once again, we were back to that place where I thought we needed to be away from home for a bit before we could come back to how we were. It doesn't make any sense to me now, but it made all the sense in the world when I was in the middle of it. I thought maybe Phil would do better if we went to the shore for a couple days, and that Toby and I would also do better at the beach—because, after all, everything seems so much better at the beach.

Those same emotions found me just a few weeks later, when Phil was released from the hospital that second time, after his first round of ECT treatments. Once again, he wasn't ready to be home—and once again, I was determined to make another misstep: after our little trip to the shore with Toby had proved ineffective, I got to thinking Phil and I needed to get away, just the two of us, so I hastily arranged for a weekend away. Looking back, I've got no idea what the heck I was thinking, sending us off on a road trip at such a vulnerable time, but I'm like a lioness when I set my mind to something. It was the first weekend after Phil came back from the hospital that second time, and it was way too soon to be taking a trip, but I was determined. I asked Phil's mother to look after Toby, and planned a getaway for us to a romantic bed-and-breakfast in New Hope, Pennsylvania. The brochure seemed great. We could eat some great food, go antiquing, take in the sights, enjoy the great outdoors and each other, at long last. Or that was the plan, at least. Truth was, Phil *so* wasn't ready to do anything of the sort. He was still struggling to speak in full sentences, still spotty on his memory, still unable to order from a menu or to cross a busy street with any kind of confidence. Don't get me wrong, he was ten times better than he'd been, but he was having trouble with some real simple stuff.

Even so, the weekend got off to a great start. We both got ready for a nice dinner at the inn, and I can't tell you how thrilled I was to sit in candlelight with my husband, to eat fantastic food together, to have some time to ourselves. We moved slowly, talking at length about our future and our family and everything we'd set aside these past months. It was beautiful, just beautiful. I think my cheeks hurt from smiling too much.

The next morning, however, my smile quickly faded— and for reasons having nothing to do with Phil, at first. At six a.m. we were awakened by a flock of geese that seemed to be holding a meeting outside our window. In an instant, they were gone, only to return fifteen minutes later. Apparently, there was a neighboring farmer who had just cut the hay on his land, and the geese were alighting outside the inn as a kind of pit stop on their way south. This went on every fifteen minutes or so, as a new group landed to replace the one that just left, and by eight thirty I was ready to climb out of my skin. Miraculously, we enjoyed about a half hour of blessed silence, but as soon as we went back to sleep there was the roar of a tractor from a nearby field.

I was already operating without a whole lot of sleep, a condition that had seemed to build and hold steady for the previous year or so, so I guess I was a little on edge. Phil, too, appeared rattled by the constant commotion, but the tractor noise just put me over the top. I threw off the covers and announced I'd had enough. "Let's go for a drive!" I said to Phil. "If I have to stay in this room another minute, I think I'll scream."

We grabbed a quick bite and ventured out to some of the antique shops in the area, just over the bridge from our inn. At our very first stop, Phil said he wanted to hang back outside for a bit, so I went in to have a look around, but when I came back Phil was really confused and out of sorts. I asked what I could do to help him, but he couldn't tell me what was wrong. The words came out all jumbled, and he had this look of panic on his face. I didn't read too much into it, because he'd been in this kind of fog before, and his doctors had always told us to just be patient with him until he could see his way clear to the other side of whatever it was, so we went to get a cup of coffee. By the third antique store, though, he looked like he was zoned out—completely not there—and I felt the smile from the night before wilt into a thousand tears.

So what did we do? We hightailed it back to the inn, and by then it was early afternoon and all these other noises had subsided, so we decided to take a nap. The room had already been made up, and the peace and quiet were just too inviting. It's always a delicious, peaceful thing, to steal a nap in the middle of a bright fall afternoon, in a freshly made bed, so we got under the covers and hoped to make the best of it. There was nothing romantic about our returning to bed, no need to read between the lines. We still hadn't gotten to that place in Phil's healing where we could try being intimate with each other. That would take another while, and that was just as well. But at just that moment we were both so bone tired that a nap seemed like the perfect escape from a day that had gotten off to a rocky start, and yet as soon as our heads hit the pillows the tractor started up again. I thought, *Argghhhh!* And then I thought this must be some kind of sign. I'm a big believer in signs, and this wasn't a good one, that I can tell you. I got it loud and clear that it was too soon to steal away on a romantic weekend, too soon to drag Phil to the countryside, in and out of overstuffed antique stores, beyond his comfortable, familiar environment. I might have very much needed to get away, after the ordeal of these past months, but Phil very much needed to be back on the unit for those additional three treatments.

In any case, there was a lot of work ahead of us, and we couldn't just "escape" into the Pennsylvania countryside and pretend that everything was all right and that Phil was as good as new, so that weekend really stood out as a harbinger of things to come. Clearly, Phil wasn't done with the ECT—or the ECT wasn't done with him. He needed to go back to Nine Garden North for a couple more treatments, and we tried to keep a positive view of this latest development. It would have been so easy to take a hangdog, defeatist approach, and to make like the shock treatments had failed and that our situation was more desperate now than ever before, but I tried to keep us in a positive place. I presented it to Phil and to our friends and family like we were just going back to top off the treatment, to put a kind of spit shine on Phil and dot all his i's and cross all his t's. That was the spin. And it wasn't just spin. It was a desperately hoped-for truth. It's what we all needed to believe.

Back at the hospital, it was a whole new race against time with the insurance company. Phil was scheduled for three additional ECT treatments, and we had maxed out his coverage. If he needed another few days in the hospital to get back up to speed after his final treatment, the insurance wouldn't cover his room on the unit, and I tried not to stress about it because we had no choice, but nevertheless it loomed as a constant worry. I should have been at Phil's side whenever I was with him at the hospital, holding his hand and guiding him through this nightmare in whatever loving ways I could manage, but there were times when I was so fixed on this insurance mess that I couldn't think of much else.

This time around, we'd only been away from Nine Garden North for a couple weeks, but there were a whole bunch of new patients on the unit when Phil returned. Some of the same folks were still there, but there'd naturally been some turnover. The staff, of course, was all in place, and some of the nurses and attendants were happy to see Phil. Clearly, they weren't *happy* to learn he hadn't chased his depression away, but he was a good guy to have around the unit. One of the nurses came by as soon as he checked back in to make sure he'd brought his guitar.

I tried not to think about these last few treatments. I'd been all caught up in them the first time around, and they'd taken so much out of me that my approach on this second pass was to just chill. We'd been down this road before, I told myself. It was no biggie. (In truth, it was the biggest of *biggies*, but I had to psyche myself down to where I wouldn't get all weirded out about them all over again.)

And Phil shouldered them fairly well. He made his steady improvements. He muddled through the fog those few hours after each treatment, and kept clawing his way back to whole, and one day I looked up and he was more like the old Phil than I could have reasonably hoped.

Dr. Wharton and Dr. Stefanovic were extremely encouraging. In fact, everybody who was involved in Phil's care was tremendous, and after another three treatments the talk turned once again to Phil's release, and this time there were no nagging doubts or uncertainties. This time, he was ready.

He came home for good on Halloween. October 31, 2003. Toby was dressed like a little lion. I was done up like a runway-model version of Morticia Addams: black wig, white face, bloodred lips. (I know, I know . . . that makes two Addams Family references, but I suppose there's no better archetype when you're writing a book about mental illness in a family setting.) The leaves were changing colors, and the air was crisp and cool, and we sat on the front steps of our house and counted our blessings. I took Toby down the street to do some trick-or-treating, and Phil wanted to just hang back and watch all the kids and parents parade through our neighborhood, and at some point I looked over my shoulder and caught a glimpse of him handing out some candy to some kids and allowed myself to think the worst of it was behind us.

It was a beautiful fall day, like something out of a Hallmark card, but the incongruity of it was startling. Phil seemed so fragile, but at the same time he was going through all these normal motions, just like every other dad in the neighborhood, hanging out in front of his house, handing out candy, and I wanted so much for Phil to finally be just like every other dad in the neighborhood that I looked past his lapses. In truth, he was still struggling. In truth, he was having trouble finding the right words to make himself understood. In truth, he had that faraway look in his eyes that I had come to associate with his depression. And yet, he was working on it. He was giving it his best shot, and as I watched him from the corner of my eye, beneath my Morticia Addams wig, I recognized this for the supremely strange moment that it was. I also recognized that Phil had never really had the chance to be that kind of father to Toby. He'd started struggling with the chronic pain when she was just a couple months old, and it had been downhill from there, and it was only now, after the uphill climb of the ECT and three stints on the psychiatric unit, that I allowed myself to think we might make it back to the top of the hill.

The next couple weeks were a little disquieting, to say the very least. It's like we took that surreal Halloween moment and layered in all these other shades of black. Jonathan was fading fast, and Phil's whole family was caught up in preparing for his death and saying their good-byes. It was such a sad, sad time, and it's like there wasn't room in all that sadness to continue feeling sad about Phil, so everyone moved about like he was in the clear. After all, he was through with his treatments and home from the hospital, so we took turns convincing ourselves he was all better, so our hearts wouldn't have to break for two brothers at the same time. But he wasn't all better, not yet, and I don't think I helped matters by willing him back to whole. It's like I was on a different planet, not knowing what Phil could handle, not knowing where we were with this thing, but wanting desperately to be normal once again.

Understand, no one wanted "normal" more than Phil, and after he was home a couple months he got it in his head that his medications were holding him back. After everything we'd been through, this struck me as perhaps the most troubling development of all, the way he seemed unable to stay on top of his medications. It's like he resented having to take them, and I was in no position to blame him on this one, but I was certainly in a position to worry. He'd have a beer or a drink from time to time, and I used to get on him about it because he knew full well that the alcohol killed the effectiveness of his meds, but it's like he didn't care. Or he cared, but he didn't care enough to do anything about it. He kept saying things like "I'm going to get off these meds." And I kept saying, "No, you're not. Not so fast. Someday, maybe, but right now, every time you open your medicine cabinet you curse at your pills. You want them to go away. But without them, you wouldn't be here. These are the things that are keeping you alive."

I'll let Phil tell the rest of it, but I don't want to close my contribution without admitting that I still don't fully trust that he's better. It's a painful thing to admit, but I do so because I think it's important. It might be helpful to other people whose partners are just coming out of a depression to know that even after almost two years, in the back of my mind, I get an image of Phil trying to kill himself if we have an argument, of me pushing him unknowingly to some unimaginable brink. Deep down, in those places we don't like to talk about, a part of me thinks, *Well, if this happened once, it could happen again.* I catch myself wondering if the depression compromised him in some permanent way, or I start to think maybe he's "faking" how well he's doing and setting us up for some other, greater fall. I guess it means I'm not completely healed myself, because I know on a rational level that he's doing great. He looks amazing, works out regularly, takes his medicines, the whole deal. He's social again, and connecting with people, and calmer and more even-keeled than he was before the depression. We're even making love again, and there's a sweet, knowing tenderness between us that I could never have imagined prior to this ordeal.

But it *is* like I'm expecting the bottom to drop out of our lives all over again, and it's something I've got to work through on my own, because the truth is we're ready for it if it does indeed come looking for us a second time. We know what to do. And we know we'll be okay.

Signs

PHIL

The line I used when I had to tell people I was going back to Nine Garden North for those additional three ECT treatments was that I wasn't fully cooked. I made a joke out of it, which I guess was the only way to deal with it. I learned that from Jonathan, watching him persevere for all those years. You have to laugh. And you have to *keep* laughing, and hoping for the best. (He called it "keeping your sense of tumor.") I could have been dejected, going back onto that unit, but I made the most of it. I can still remember bursting through those double doors after being gone those few weeks, and seeing my old friend Barnes on the unit, and spreading my arms wide and announcing, "I'm back." Like I was a guest on some variety show or something. And Barnes—bless him—took one look at me and knew how tough it must have been to have to come back to the hospital like that, and he said, "That's okay, Phil.

You're going to be all right. Don't worry. Good to see you, man."

And it was good to be seen. It truly was. Sure, it would have been better to be seen under some other set of circumstances—say, as a *visitor* on the unit instead of as a *patient*—but I felt safe around these people. I felt like this was where I needed to be in order to get where I wanted to go, if that makes any sense. So, yeah, in this one respect anyway, it was good to be back, and I completed my additional three treatments like I had them coming, and I went home that Halloween, and at some point I looked up and realized the time had come to jump-start the rest of my life. I was feeling much, much better, even if I wasn't quite back to being myself. I was still feeling out of it, still unable to completely express my thoughts. And I was still unable to remember bits and pieces of what had happened as recently as the day before, but I wanted to hop back onto life's treadmill and start experiencing things again, wanting to get back to it, and knowing that the only way there was to keep pushing myself.

Like Emme, I'm a big believer in signs, and I was about to bump into three really big ones. The first was the biggest of all: in January 2004, Jonathan finally lost his battle to brain cancer. We were all with him when he died, and it was so desperately and overwhelmingly sad, but we'd had seventeen years to brace for this moment, and I think we came through it pretty well.

This isn't a book about Jonathan; I'll save that for another day. But I do want to emphasize how much a part of me he is, how connected we will always be to each other, and how much his heroic struggle made mine look like chickenfeed. Man, this guy was absolutely incredible, the way he faced his illness. He was the real deal. Here's one final Jonathan story, just to get the point across: a week or two after he first started a new round of radiation treatments, Jonathan went out to a party. He didn't care how sick he was, how dire his prognosis—if there was a good party going on, he wanted to be there. His thinking was, *Hey, I'm alive. Might as well make the best of it.* The reality was, on this one night anyway, he was feeling pretty lousy, but I guess he figured once he got out and about his adrenaline would get going and he'd start feeling better. Anyway, he got to the party, and he started hanging with his friends. At some point, he started dancing, and while he was dancing he started to sweat, so he naturally brought his forearm to his head and kind of wiped at his brow. We've all done it, only in this case, Jonathan pulled back his arm and noticed a clump of his hair stuck to it, so he fussed with his hair for a bit, and more clumps started to come out. So what did he do? He raced back to his apartment, quickly shaved his head, and then raced back to the party, bald as a cue ball. That's the kind of guy he was—brave and wild and crazy and able to shoulder absolutely anything. Even the idea that his big brother might try to kill himself.

Okay, so here's the big sign. As soon as Jonathan died—almost to the very moment he drew his last breath—I was suffused with this great strength and spirit. *His* strength and spirit, I felt sure of it. Really, it's like his giant wellspring of energy needed a place to park itself, and it looked to me, and I was buoyed by it. It sounds corny, I know, and impossible to believe, but there it was and there was no denying it. When I awoke the next morning, my depression just fell away; I felt completely and unmistakably like my old self. Talk about a sign, right? It was just incredible, almost like a light went out for Jonathan just as a new one decided to shine for me, and of course Emme and I didn't trust it at first; we didn't know if it was a fleeting response to Jonathan's death, or a momentary high like I used to experience when I was playing around with my medications. There could have been any number of explanations for it, and yet, with each passing day, there it would remain. I realize now of course that there are probably a dozen more rational explanations for it. It was just ten weeks or so since my final ECT treatments, and maybe it had taken all this time for the dust to settle in my brain and for the cobwebs to clear and for me to start feeling right. Or maybe the meds had finally kicked in and started doing what they were meant to do all along. Or maybe it was a combination of the ECT therapy and the medication. Or maybe the depression had simply run its course. But I like to think Jonathan had a hand in it, and that he was watching over me. It's like that dream I had, when I was on the psych unit, when the healthy Jonathan was pushing the sick Jonathan in his wheelchair and turning to me and telling me everything was going to be okay. I kept having that dream, and maybe this was why.

Everyone we knew turned out for the funeral. It was something to see. We had Jonathan dressed in a James Taylor baseball cap and sunglasses. We all thought that would be kind of cool. My mother was all upset because she couldn't find a favorite jacket of Jonathan's that he wanted to be buried in, and a couple months later she came across it and went out to the cemetery and dug a small hole with a little gardening shovel she'd brought from home and stuffed the jacket inside.

We sat shiva—the Jewish period of mourning—at Seth's house, and it was such an emotionally conflicted period in our lives, because I was feeling healthy and whole, for the first time in two and a half years, and underneath all of that there was this giant sadness, a gaping hole where Jonathan had been. There was a lot of laughing and reminiscing, which was good, and there was a lot of crying and hugging, which was also good. I went to temple, to recite the Mourner's Kaddish, and I stood outside myself a little bit, not willing to believe that I was actually standing in temple, saying Kaddish for my little brother.

If I dwelled on it for too long, I would have crumpled to the floor in sorrow, but I knew Jonathan was in a much better place—and, now, so was I. It was strange, because I couldn't really talk to anyone other than Emme about how I was feeling, not just yet. I didn't think anyone would understand, and more than that I didn't want to distract anyone from mourning. This time was all about Jonathan, I realized, and it thrilled me to realize it because I knew that this too was an indication of my sudden improvement. I was attuned to everything, at long last, and I remember thinking, *God, I've missed this.* And, *This is what it's like to be alive.*

Finally.

The killing side to this sudden turn was that the burning sensation in my prostate area flared up again, pretty
much coinciding with Jonathan's death. Amazingly, it had
never been diagnosed until this new episode. In all that
time, reaching back nearly two years, I never had an MRI
or a CAT scan, and when the intense pain surfaced again
after my depression had finally lifted, a friend suggested I
consult a radiologist. I had a whole new attitude about
pain management, and proactive care, and this was my
first chance to put it to the test. It was January 2004, and
to this day I don't know what took me so long—but hey,
better late than never, right? I landed in the office of Dr.
David Habif, a radiologist who had previously treated my
brother Jonathan. Dr. Habif did a CAT scan of my
prostate and concluded without hesitation that I had a
"raging" case of prostatitis, and I look back now and wonder what the hell I was thinking, to put off such a basic di-
agnostic test for so long. It should have been the first step
I took in my treatment, instead of the last straw. Again, if
I had it to do differently, I'd have gotten a CAT scan or an
MRI right away.

I'd never heard of prostatitis hitting a man my age, and
I wondered if Dr. Habif thought it might still be the pelvic
pain syndrome that had been diagnosed all those months
earlier. "Phil," he said, "what's pelvic pain syndrome?"
That gives you an idea how frustrating it was to get everyone on the same page—doctors, no less!—and to have that
page correspond at least in some way to a page in a medical
text. It also gives you an idea how hungry I was for validation, that the pain I was experiencing was all too real. It

took Dr. Habif to finally tell me, "Hey, Phil, you're not crazy." The pain might have driven me crazy, but at least now I knew it was real. At least now it had a name.

Prostatitis is an inflammation of the prostate gland that results in the burning pain I'd been experiencing, and the diagnosis seemed to match up with my symptoms and my history. Plus, Dr. Habif showed me the film from the scan, and I could see quite clearly that the gray areas that indicated swelling almost completely covered my prostate. At long last, we were on to something—and I wondered how all these other doctors could have missed it, when it now appeared so obvious—but at this late date the diagnosis seemed almost beside the point.

Anyway, the prostatitis had been gone for about a year, and here it was again, as if from nowhere. Nobody could tell me if there was an emotional trigger, but I started to experience some of that same intense burning, the same pain when I went to the bathroom. It wasn't as bad as it had been the first time around, but I was determined not to let it get out of control, so I got on the phone immediately with Dr. Wharton and demanded that he give me the most serious pain medication his little computer program would recommend alongside all the antidepressants he still had me taking, because I really wanted to kick this thing in the butt before it could knock me on mine.

Feb. 9, '04

It's been a long time since I've written in this journal. I'm back mentally! Jan. 7, Dad's 66th birthday, was the day. Jonathan passed on the 6th of January. I know through the grace of God his strength was given to me. Jonathan gave me his strength! I'm still dealing with the pain below but I'm on pain meds and it's not going to bring me down this time. I have it licked. No more depression! Must get pain under control and I'll truly be back.

As it turned out, this final round of penile pain only lasted for a few weeks, and even as I was in the middle of it, I remember thinking it was a good trade, the depression for the pain. Two and a half years earlier, when this whole ordeal started, I had thought the pain was unbearable, and I couldn't imagine anything worse, but now I had some perspective on it. Now I'd been depressed. And now I welcomed it, if it meant the depression would go away, and stay away.

The second big sign actually found me before the first, but it wasn't quite so big as losing Jonathan, and so it falls to second position here. It started when Seth ran into an old high school friend we hadn't seen in years. Her name was Peggy. She was a year ahead of me at Syracuse after high school. We'd see each other from time to time, but hadn't for the longest while. Peggy ran a company that sold promotional products and premium incentive items—putting logos on T-shirts and hats and pens and calculators . . . that sort of thing. She and Seth spent a few minutes chatting, and at one point, she asked Seth how I was doing.

"Don't ask," he said.

"What's the matter?" Peggy wanted to know.

"Well," Seth said, "he's in a really bad way. He's in a depression. He tried to commit suicide."

Peggy was taken completely aback, and was immediately concerned. Most people, when you tell them your identical twin brother is in a depression, they look for the nearest exit, because people just don't want to talk about stuff like this, but Peggy was not like most people. She told Seth that she had suffered through a serious bout of postpartum depression and that she knew exactly what I must be going through, and as soon as she found out I was home and not knowing what to do with my time, she insisted I come to work for her. She said I needed to get out of the house, and do something completely different, to shake me out of what was left of my depression.

It was like a godsend, although Emme didn't see it that way at first. She thought it was too soon for me to be out of the house, working, going out on sales calls, and she might have been right, but I was a stubborn son of a bitch when I got my head around something. It was just a month or two after I'd come home from my final ECT treatment, and I was still very much out of it. Compared to the miracle progress I would make the night Jonathan died, I still had a desperately long way to go, but nevertheless the idea of a new job held enormous appeal. Unfortunately, I was one of the few people who saw it this way.

One of the things that had Emme on edge about the job was the way it would leave me out there and vulnerable. My mother was concerned about this, too. Being a salesperson is tough enough when you're coming at it from a healthy place; when you're coming at it fresh off a depression, the constant rejection can be a worrisome thing. But I wasn't too worried about that. My only concern was getting myself out the door and to a first meeting with Peggy. I was supposed to head out to a diner in Tenafly to meet with her over break-fast, to talk about what the job might look like—and I almost couldn't drag myself out of the car. Seth had set the whole thing up, and I called him on the phone, wanting to bail on him.

I said, "Oh, my God, I can't go. I just can't."

He said, "Why not?"

I said, "I don't know. I just can't."

He said, "You're going."

I said, "Seth, I'm sick. I've got a stomach virus. I don't want to get her sick."

Some bullshit line.

He said, "Phil, I'm coming over. I'll walk you out of the car and into the diner myself."

I don't know how, but I managed to cross the parking lot and go inside the diner to meet with Peggy, and after we caught up with each other she told me all about the oppor-tunity she had for me. It sounded great. Her company—Arthur Kermit Associates, which was started by her grandfather—had a strong line of fun products that almost sold themselves. It was absolutely something I could do, and do well, and the closer I got to it the more I realized it would give me some purpose and some all-important struc-ture, so I signed on. I worked for commission, so it's not like Peggy would be out any money if things didn't work out. She'd give me an office, and a line of products to sell, and maybe some leads, and the rest would be up to me. If I

could make a good go of it, that'd be great. If I couldn't . . .
well, at least I would have tried, so I set about it.

Understand, the idea of me getting back to work was
very much front and center in our household. Despite her
concerns about me going into sales, Emme kept pushing
me to get back to work in her own not-so-subtle ways, and
in my own not-so-subtle ways I kept resisting it, but it
was clearly time. Trouble was, Emme's not-so-subtle push
seemed to also be showing me the door, in terms of my involvement with Emme Associates. While I was in the hospital, she moved our offices out of the house and into a
professional building in town. The move made a lot of sense
(we needed the extra room in the house, and Emme thought
if we had a more professional space we could more easily
grow the business), but I didn't even hear about it until I
was home, and it left me feeling like I was being put out and
cast away. We never really talked about it, but there were all
these hints, all around, and I came to realize that I no longer
had a place in our "family business." (A business I helped
to build!) I wasn't strong enough emotionally to be upset or
indignant over this, but it did leave me feeling a little abandoned.

The more I thought about it, though, the more I realized
Emme was right to encourage me in a new direction. She believed it was important to put some kind of buffer between
our home lives and our professional lives; even when I was
completely healthy, when we were working together and
things were going great, it had been impossible to shut off
one valve for the sake of the other. Now, though, as I began
to recognize a need to do *something* with all my bottled-up

creative and professional energy, she felt I needed to be able to get away from work at the end of each day, to decompress. She wasn't happy about me taking a sales job, because I'd be open to constant rejection, but she wasn't about to talk me down from it. A job was a job, and I got it in my head that this was something I wanted to try.

Trouble was, I sometimes had a tough time getting started, chasing down a new lead. For no real reason, I'd catch myself staring off into space when I should have been making phone calls. Or I'd drive to an appointment—yes, I was driving again!—and pull into the parking lot and sit in the car for a ridiculously long time before heading inside to make the sales call. Sometimes, I'd crank the seat back and hang there for so long that I'd fall asleep. One morning, I pulled into the parking lot of a Drug Fair pharmacy, in a suit and tie, and I nodded off in the car, procrastinating, and when I woke up with a start it was after noon—that's how tough it was to get started, making these cold calls, the same way it was tough to get myself out the door and over to that diner to meet with Peggy in the first place.

Understand, I was feeling so much better by this point. The depression had pretty much lifted, but I was still somewhat fragile, and tentative. Whatever confidence I'd had before the depression, it would take time to rediscover. I wasn't quite the balls-to-the-wall soul I used to be, the guy who never took no for an answer. Not just yet.

But I pushed myself. And Seth helped with the pushing. He kept sending me these great leads, and the deeper I got into it, the more I realized I was enjoying myself. The job called on some of my creativity, which had pretty much been lying dormant for the past couple years. It allowed me to match a company's image and sensibility with a thousand or so different "branded" products, and to give things a new, fun twist. Very quickly, I spent less and less time procrastinating, and more and more time coming up with new strategies and ideas, and going out on calls.

And I was starting to make *some* money—at long last. It's been suggested to me that perhaps the fact that I was finally contributing to our household finances might have contributed in some way to my healing, but I don't buy it. With us, it was never about *yours* or *mine*, just *ours.* It didn't matter who earned the money, just that we had enough coming in to allow us to do the things we wanted to do. And so, no, it wasn't about the money. It was about starting to get my mojo back, and moving about with the confidence I had known all along. The "Positive Phil" I pretended to be when I did that alphabet exercise on the psych unit all those months earlier was finally the Positive Phil I saw looking back at me in the mirror each morning.

It was one of Seth's leads that took me to my third big sign—and this one just about killed me. (Really, really.) This one happened several months after I took the job with Arthur Kermit Associates. I was shooting out on Route 78 West, out by Newark Airport, off to meet a guy who knew Seth and said he'd see me about a possible order. I was in my Alfa Spider, and it was the middle of the day, and there weren't too many cars on the road so I was moving at a pretty good clip, maybe seventy to seventy-five miles per hour. I was heading into a stretch of road where there's a big, grassy divider between eastbound and westbound traffic, almost like it's two separate highways. The next thing I knew, my car was spinning out of control, and as I was spinning I had time to think of the irony in my situation. Someone had hit me from behind, on the back quarter panel, driver's side, and sent me into a spin. There I was, about to crash at high speed in my little red Spider convertible, which of course was what I had so desperately wanted to do a year or so earlier, driving up and down the Palisades Parkway with my eyes closed at even greater speeds—only now, I didn't want to die. I wanted to *live*!

The car did two complete revolutions, and it was like I was moving in slow motion. It happened too fast to think about it, too fast to do anything about it, but at the same time things were unraveling in this painstaking way. Spinning, I flashed on an image of me on one of those cup-and-saucer-type rides at an amusement park; that's what I was thinking of. As I spun, the car skidded off the road, but not before a big semi roared by perilously close to me—and missed me, literally, by inches. I was petrified, and yet there was something weirdly soothing about it, too, when the truck buzzed past and I realized it wouldn't hit me, because I wasn't so far removed from that time in my life when I would have welcomed the collision. Let me tell you, the moment was so thick with irony it's a wonder the irony didn't slow me down and keep the car from spinning.

I finally came to rest in a grassy area full of shrubs and bushes, the car buried up to its belly in a patch of grass and dried mud, and as I climbed out of the car there was dirt and grass and debris on my face, and twigs and leaves in my hair, but I basically didn't have a scratch on me. The Alfa was in fairly good shape, too, considering—the rear bumper was torn off, and she was a little dirtied up, and scratched here and there, with a dent the size of a basketball on that rear panel, but other than that there was no significant body damage, and as I stepped away from the car I looked up to the sky and said a silent prayer: *"Thank you, God."* And then another: *"Thank you, Jonathan."*

I called a tow truck, and waited around on the side of the highway for these guys to come and put the car on a flatbed and haul it out to the body shop, and to give me a ride along the way, and as I waited I caught myself thinking that Jonathan had once again had a hand in saving me from myself. I really felt this way—truly and wholeheartedly. He was looking out for me, an angel on my shoulder. I was his big brother, and I should have been there to look out for him the last few years of his life, but he had my back just the same.

And then for some reason I thought back to the very first person I ever knew who committed suicide. I was in eleventh grade, and our high school was buzzing one morning about one of our classmates who had shot himself in the head over a drug deal gone bad. Or maybe it was a runaway gambling debt. I never learned the particulars of the event beyond all of our teenage speculation, but it was abundantly clear that this kid had blown his brains out and that I would never see him again. That's all that registered. His gym locker was directly across from mine. We never hung out, but we were always friendly toward each other. He was a big, gentle giant, probably the last person I'd have pegged to get involved in such a heavy-duty way with drugs or gambling or whatever it was that ultimately drove him to kill himself.

I felt so empty when I heard the news. I wondered why he hadn't gone to his parents, or to a teacher, or to a friend. Yes, he was probably in a mess of trouble, but I'm sure his parents would have rather been pissed at their son than have to attend his funeral. I kept coming back to the idea that if this kid had reached out to someone, he might still be here today. Suicide is not the answer. It wasn't the answer for me, and it wasn't the answer for this kid back in high school. It's a permanent solution to a temporary problem. There is no coming back. There is no second chance. It's final, a done deal, over and out. It pains me now to think that I too wanted to take my own life, that I was prepared to leave Emme without a husband and Toby without a father. That's why I'm so proactive now whenever I hear of someone who's in trouble, because most times if you can just get past these trouble spots, you'll be okay. Nothing is worth taking your life.

You know, back when I was in Nine Garden North, my mind kept bouncing to an old Merv Griffin interview I remembered from when I was a kid. (It's funny, the things you remember, when you can't even remember who'd been by to visit you the night before.) Merv had Mr. T on the show as his guest—this was when *The A-Team* was a big hit and Mr. T was one of the biggest things going—and Merv asked Mr. T what he would do if someone held him up and told him to give him all the gold he had hanging around his neck.

I guess Merv was baiting Mr. T into one of his trademark "I pity the fool" routines, and like everyone else, I expected him to say he would crush anyone who dared to mess with him. But Mr. T surprised me. He said, "I'd give them all my money, gold, whatever I had that was worth anything."

Merv said, "Why?"

Mr. T said, "You don't cry over something that can't cry over you."

I thought that was pretty cool, and intelligent, and the exchange stayed with me over the years because it reminded me that life was so fragile and precious, and that we are here on this earth for but a moment. And so I urge all of you, if you've been with us on this journey and you find yourself heading down a similar road, get help. Talk to someone—a parent, a teacher, a doctor, a friend, a priest, a rabbi . . . anyone. When I was struggling through my depression, I never thought I'd get out of it. I felt that the hole I was in was far too deep for me to ever climb back out to the top. But how lucky I was to have family and friends and doctors toss enough dirt in the hole that I could regain my footing and reach the edge and climb out!

Now that I'm out, and whole, and my feet are planted firmly on the ground, I'm able to look back and marvel at what I've been through. I think, *Hey, I made it up and out—* not exactly unscathed, but I'm still here so I'm not about to quibble. The positive spin on my two-and-a-half-year struggle with depression is that it's enabled me to reach out and help others. Strike that, it's *obligated* me to reach out and help others. That's the way I feel, like it's my small price to pay for making it out alive, and the least I can do to balance the karmic scales.

I realize now that I was so self-absorbed during my

depression it's a wonder all my friends and family stuck it out with me. I hear back some of the things I used to say, or think through some of the ways I interacted with people, and I get sick to my stomach. *I, I, I . . . Me, me, me . . . When am I going to get better? When am I going to be me again?* I don't look at my life in just this way anymore, and it's not just because I'm no longer depressed. I've had a real shift in perspective, almost like I've been away to some cruel finishing school and sent home with all this knowledge and insight and wisdom. That's a funny way to look at what I've been through, like it's been an education:

Hey, Phil, what have you been up to these past couple years?

Well, funny you should ask. I've been studying depression . . . the real way.

Life is experience and experience is life—and both are crazy and unpredictable. As I sit here in my backyard, putting the finishing touches to these pages, everywhere I look I'm reminded of how uncertain our time on this earth can be. It can be a glorious day, but there are always storms on the horizon. Even as I write this, I can hear the sound of a chain saw in the distance: town crews cleaning up trees and branches that fell in a flash thunderstorm the other day. The noise reminds me how one minute everything can be fine and dandy and the next minute all hell can break loose. You just never know. If you'd have told me my brother Jonathan would die from brain cancer, I would have had *you* committed to a psychiatric unit. Or that my brother Seth would struggle with depression. Or that I would be in a horrific depression of my own—for two and a half years!—one that pushed me to try to take my own life.

It reminds me of a poem I wrote back in high school, which I still keep in my desk drawer:

IF
The uncertainty of life is if
What one encounters is unknown
Through miracle of birth some obtain more than others
Yet, their fate is not secure
Forces beyond control determine life
What if one performed acts differently?
There would still be an if.
If sleep is endless where might one be?
Only death is certain there is no if.

I read over what I wrote all those years ago and try to reconcile it with the experiences of the past few years. Uncertain? You bet. Forces beyond my control? Absolutely. But underneath all of that uncertainty and helplessness there was Emme. She took care of me. She jumped out of her life to take care of mine. It's amazing what good people can do when struck with adversity, what reserves of strength they can tap into when someone they love is in distress. I know there were times during my depression that Emme was so angry and frustrated she probably just wanted to kill me. (Well, *that* would have solved at least a few of my problems!) But all kidding aside, it takes a special someone, with tremendous strength of character and heart and conviction and pure, boundless devotion to "Stand by Your Man" the way Emme stood by me. I don't think I can ever express to her how much her love, concern, persistence and faith helped to pull me through. I can tell her in person, or write about it here, or shout it from the rooftops and still never get the message across. She had her moments of doubt, as she has shared here, but she never lost hope that the man she married would eventually come back to her. A part of her knew we would all wake from this nightmare and move forward, leaving the bad dream behind.

And do you know what? As difficult and as painful as my life had become during the depression, I can look back on that period and gain strength from it, knowing that everything I went through, good and bad, helped bring me to where I am today. We've all heard that old expression— what doesn't kill you can only make you stronger. Well, the depression couldn't kill me. *I* couldn't kill me. And here I am, stronger for having climbed my way back out.

Starting Over

It'd be great if I could put a neat bow on things and say that the old Phil came roaring back once his depression lifted, but that's not how it happened. (I wish!) Don't get me wrong, Phil was truly transformed—overnight, it seemed—but there was still a long way for us to go before we were back to where we had been. There was a period of adjustment, in the weeks following Jonathan's death, during which Phil was a little bit out of control—drinking, even though he knew it killed the effectiveness of his antidepressants; skipping meds, even though he knew he needed to maintain the fine balance his doctors had prescribed if they were to have any chance of working; running on and on about how he hated the crutch of his medications and vowing to take himself off of them, even though he knew he would likely be on some form of antidepressant for the rest of his life.

I went from being gratified at seeing some of Phil's familiar pluck and gumption to being baffled. I had thought all that negative stuff would be behind us, but it flitted in and out of our lives for the next while. I understood deep down that Phil was just trying to climb back up and into his life in whatever ways he could, and that he was grabbing at anything, but his behavior could be unsettling. In postdepression, he sometimes spoke harshly, or blamed me for things he knew full well had nothing to do with me, but I tried to let it all slide. I tried to remember and keep close that this was all part of the arc of his healing.

Together, we slipped into this postdepression phase, which is a whole other ball of wax that nobody told us about. You'd think, after all that time in the hospital, with all these doctors, somebody might have warned us of the tense moments still ahead of us, but I guess everyone was so concerned about dragging Phil from the depths of his depression and praying for some kind of light at the end of the tunnel that nobody paid much attention to how we'd all manage once we actually *saw* the light at the end of the tunnel. (First things first, right?) Some days, Phil seemed to be mad at me, for no apparent reason. Other days, he seemed to be mad at himself, also for no apparent reason. Some days, he was mad at the world, about his depression, or Jonathan, or whatever. His moods weren't necessarily tied to anything that had passed between us, or to how his day was going; they would just seem to wash over him, unannounced and unexplained. I found myself looking back, at all the time we spent together *before* the depression, all the years we'd been married, and realized that there had always been an element of these weird mood shifts in our relationship, so I figured we'd use this postdepression period as an opportunity to work on some of these things—and we have, to our great and (hopefully) lasting benefit.

One of the great boosts I had in this area was my relationship with a therapist of my very own, who I began seeing in June 2004, hoping to deal with the anger I apparently felt over Phil's suicide attempt, and his inexplicably surly and moody behavior that began to surface postdepression. I found myself wondering when I would ever get my husband back. My anger would bubble forth in my conversations with Phil, almost on its own, and I wanted to get a handle on it before it got away from us. And I did. I came to realize that it was natural and human for me to be pissed at Phil on some level, but that I also needed to find ways to forgive him. At the same time, I needed to find a way to deal with the anger Phil was expressing, and his frustration at how to jump-start his life beneath the regimen of all those medications, many of which still carried some unpleasant side effects. I even had to adjust to how he was parenting Toby, because of course I had done almost all of the parenting for most of her little life, and once Phil was back in the picture we had to reimagine a great many of our household routines. He was learning how to be a dad, and I was learning how to keep my mouth shut—I guess that's the most *political* way to put it.

Another great boost was that I finally found time for myself. For two and a half years our lives had been all about Phil's illness. First it was that odd, Epstein-Barr-like virus, and then it was the chronic pain that we finally diagnosed as prostatitis, and then it was the depression. There had been no time for me . . . until now. As soon as Phil was doing better and better, I began stealing these little pockets of time to reconnect with the parts of my life that had been dormant. I visited with girlfriends. I got caught up on all the major life-cycle events that had occupied my friends' attentions since I last checked in: births, weddings, divorces, deaths . . . I got a chance to fill folks in on what had *really* been going on with us during this time. I even picked up golf and played in a couple tournaments, got scuba certified, and completed my first triathlon. I felt like a colt in a big, open space, kicking up my heels in joyous freedom.

Phil, too, started doing some work on his new and improved self! He began seeing a new therapist—Dr. Joe Luciani—who in just a few sessions seemed to work wonders with all the issues that continued to swirl around Phil in the aftermath of his depression. He looked at how he might begin to forgive himself for trying to take his own life, and for putting all of us through the ringer, even though he knew on a rational level that there was nothing he could have done any differently.

And, most important, we found time for each other. We reignited our long-dormant tradition of a "date night," which we had had to start soon after we were married, to keep our busy lives in check and ensure that we put our relationship ahead of all else, and for the first time in too, too long we were really able to sit and have a stressless conversation. I was elated. And talk about reigniting! We started making love again, and the intimacy between us had blossomed into something wonderful and special. Now, a year and a half out, we are able to be there for each other again in this intimate way, and I'm delighted to report it's like we are experiencing a sweet extension of what we already had before. It's precious and sacred and beautiful and all those good things, and I'm so thankful to have Phil back in my life in *this* way as well as in every other way.

Really, we're light-years from how things were on that morning of August 1, 2003, when I found Phil semiconscious in our bed after taking all those pills. He's finally learned how to say no to Toby without feeling guilty about it, or caving under one of her pouty looks. He's finally able to tell me to stick it, if I come at him out of left field. (As if *that* never happened before all of this!) And there's once again room for us to joke with and tease each other, and not take everything so gosh darn seriously. We can yell and scream like any other couple—maybe even a little louder, because we know the other person won't walk away and give up. We've walked through hell together, and if we have to we'll walk through hell together all over again.

Now, on to one of the compelling side benefits of Phil's depression: as Phil got better, he felt the need to shed some firsthand light on a deadly disease that few people speak openly about. And I came to think, *Good for him.* Better, Good for all of us. Ever since he got out of the hospital, he's been like an ambassador for good mental health. People seek him out, and tell him their stories, and he tells them they're not alone. It's become his thing. He encourages these people to press on, to be aggressive in their treatment, and to lean on friends and family. He becomes their biggest supporter. Or he'll do the seeking out, if someone tells him about a relative or colleague or acquaintance who's battling depression, and share *his* story with them. It's almost like a mission with him, and it's a wonderful thing to see, how he puts himself out there in such a vulnerable way because doing so might make all the difference to someone going through what he went through.

I'm aware now that Phil and I are in a position to help a great many people—not because we know everything there is to know about depression, mind you, but because we've lived through it with war stories to share. We've come to realize that nobody knows all there is to know about depression, not even the leading experts in the field. Every depression is different, every patient is different, and every dynamic between two people is different, which is why these anecdotal accounts get passed along among patients and their families like a giant game of telephone. In fact, I believe it's our layperson's approach to Phil's illness that helps our story resonate with couples struggling through their own depressions. There is safety in numbers, absolutely, and as I read over these pages I catch myself thinking how great it would have been to have had an account like this one at our disposal when we were in the middle of it. Not to toot our own horn or anything, but I was hungry for stories of other couples' experiences, for validation that we were moving in the right direction. And, more than anything else, I needed to know that we were not alone.

And so if there's one message I want readers to take from this book, it's this: hope. Make a place for it in your life, because you're going to need it. Never lose sight of it. Know that you can make it to the other side of the darkness, just as Phil and I made it, and just as thousands of other couples make it.

Praise every morning, like it says in the Cat Stevens song that gave us the title of this book. And know that there are all kinds of people pulling for you—friends, family . . . even complete strangers who happened to go through their own version of the same ordeal and managed to see their way safely to the other side.

CLOSING THOUGHTS

Grace Notes

EMME AND PHIL

A book such as this one is not written in a vacuum, just as the lives it contains are not left to unravel in an isolated way. We walk side by side through this uncertain world, but we also stand on the shoulders of our friends and family and talented colleagues, which is why we must offer a nod to those who have helped us along the way.

To Dan Strone, our close friend and literary agent: thank you for encouraging us to face our experiences head-on, and pushing us to let go of fear and be open enough to share our toughest times with others. You made this book a reality.

To Dan Paisner, our writing partner: we are so very proud of this book, and thank you for gracing us with your incredible talent. You were the glue to our compelling story. We absolutely could not have shared it without you.

To Amy Fierro, our right arm, confidante, and eagle eye:

there are not enough words to express our gratitude for your commitment and passion. We are so lucky to have you in our lives.

To Todd Gold, for encouraging us to open up and share our story with your *People* magazine readers. The overwhelming response we received from that one article helped us decide to write this book.

To Mark Chait and his incredible NAL team—Claire Zion, Kara Welsh, Brent Howard, Donita Dooley, Craig Burke, and Anthony Ramondo: thank you for understanding the importance of sharing our journey through depression and knowing that this story was one that needed to be told. We are eternally grateful for your support.

Judy and Herman: at every turn you were right there for both of us with untiring energy and love.

Seth: we've shared so many things together but let's agree that depression doesn't have to be one of them. Okay? You're the man!

Liora, Benjamin, Arianna: your constant love and support have helped us tremendously.

Chip: you are truly a brother! Jen, Reese, Abby and Sarah, thank you.

Melanie and David: your visits, love and concern are so appreciated.

Edna and Alex: thank you for constantly reaching out.

Sally and Walter: thanks for your listening ears when the toughest times hit.

Bobbie and Eric: we are so blessed to have you in our lives.

Toby, our sweet daughter: your mere existence helped us more than you'll ever know.

And finally, to all of the police and EMT workers who responded to Emme's 911 call, and to all of the doctors and staff at Nine Garden North: thank you, thank you, thank you. Your knowledge, instincts and true concern for Phil's well-being are the reasons we are here today.

An ancient Chinese philosopher once said, "A journey of a thousand miles begins with a single step." We've indeed taken more than ten thousand steps, with support from family, friends and countless others. If we've failed to mention you in these pages, please know that we appreciate you all. We thank you from the bottoms of our hearts and wish you good health, blessings and peace always.

One final thought: our story is a story of hope. It's a story of promise. It's a story of survival. And the great thing is it's just one of many such stories that are being told each and every day, all around the world. Not all stories have a happy ending, but this one does. In fact, we can't even think of it as an ending. We still have a great many chapters to write in the story of our lives together, and we are so blessed and thankful to be able to share it with each other, with our beautiful daughter, Toby—and now, in these pages, with you. We're just getting started.

So here goes: the beginning . . .

For more information about Emme

or Emme and Phil please visit www.emmestyle.com.

Appendix

EXTRA HELP

In addition to their boundless love and support, friends and family showered us with books to help us make sense of our experience, and there were several that proved very helpful. The titles below were the best of the bunch:

Self-Coaching: How to Heal Anxiety and Depression, by Dr. Joseph J. Luciani (Wiley, 2001)

The Power of Self-Coaching: The Five Essential Steps to Creating the Life You Want, by Dr. Joseph Luciani (Wiley, 2004)

Why Suicide? Answers to 200 of the Most Frequently Asked Questions About Suicide, Attempted Suicide, and Assisted Suicide, by Eric Marcus (HarperCollins, 1996)

Darkness Visible: A Memoir of Madness, by William Styron
(Vintage, 1992)

The Power of Now: A Guide to Spiritual Enlightenment, by
Eckhart Tolle (New World Library, 1999)

*The Power of Intention: Learning to Co-Create Your World
Your Way,* by Dr. Wayne W. Dyer (Hay House, 2004)

*Restoring Intimacy: The Patients' Guide to Maintaining Re-
lationships During Depression,* by Drew Pinsky, M.D., Anita
H. Clayton, M.D., Robert M. A. Hirschfeld, M.D., Martha M.
Manning, Ph.D., Lauren Epstein Rosen, Ph.D., and Thomas
N. Wise, M.D. (Fountain Book Press, 1999)

Man's Search for Meaning, by Viktor Emil Frankl (Pocket
Books, 1997)

*Down Came the Rain: My Journey Through Postpartum
Depression,* by Brooke Shields (Hyperion, 2005)

Lost in America: A Journey with My Father, by Sherwin B.
Nuland (Knopf, 2003)

Climbing Higher, by Montel Williams (New American Library, 2004)

Beyond the printed page, there are several national organizations that offer invaluable assistance to patients suffering from depression, as well as to families and caregivers. They are:

American Association of Suicidology
5221 Wisconsin Avenue, NW
Washington, DC 20015
Phone: (202) 237-2280
Fax: (202) 237-2282
www.suicidology.org

National Mental Health Association
2001 N. Beauregard Street, 12th Floor
Alexandria, Virginia 22311
Phone: (703) 684-7722
Fax: (703) 684-5968
www.nmha.org

National Institute of Mental Health (NIMH)
Public Information and Communications Branch
6001 Executive Boulevard, Room 8184, MSC 9663
Bethesda, Maryland 20892-9663
Phone: (866) 615-6464
Fax: (301) 443-4279
www.nimh.nih.gov

Crisis Hotline Number
1-800-Suicide

ABOUT THE AUTHORS

Emme, bestselling author of *Life's Little Emergencies* and *True Beauty*, is a supermodel, TV host, and creative director of her own clothing line. She has twice been selected by *People* as one of the "50 Most Beautiful People." **Phillip Aronson** is the Visual Executive Officer of the Emme® brand, SVP of Arthur Kermit Associates, and a singer/songwriter. He performs with his identical twin brother, Seth, under the name Mirror Images. Visit their Web site at www.emme-style.com.